TRANSFORMATIONAL SELLING

TRANSFORMATIONAL SELLING

BRYN THOMPSON

STEVE LOWNDES

This edition published in Great Britain in 2023

by Bryn Thompson and Steve Lowndes

Copyright © Bryn Thompson and Steve Lowndes 2023

Bryn Thompson and Steve Lowndes have asserted their right under the Copyright, Design and Patents Act 1988 to be identified as the authors of this work.

A CIP catalogue for this book is available from the British Library.

ISBN 978-1-7392950-0-4 (pbk)

ISBN 978-1-7392950-1-1 (ebook)

Cover design by Arch Publishing Services

www.archpub.net

Printed and bound in Great Britain by Clays Ltd, Elcograf S.p.A.

CONTENTS

Foreword   vii
About the Authors   xi
Introduction   xiii

1. The Emergence of the Transformational Seller   1
2. The Behaviours of the Transformational Seller   14
3. The Customer Buying Journey   38
4. Exploding the USP Myth and the
   Transformational Difference   60
5. The Transformational Mindset   77
6. Opening Up the Opportunity   92
7. The Power of Collaborative Discovery (The
   SCOPE Model)   110
8. Qualification for the Transformational Seller   133
9. Questioning for Influence   155
10. Leveraging Expertise   177
11. Managing the Process   198
12. Pitch Perfect   214
13. A Game Both Teams Can Win   237
14. Gaining Active Commitment   261

Summary   283
Appendix A. Tier 1 Qualification. DANT   289
Appendix B: Tier 2 Qualification: CASE   293
Afterword   297
Glossary of Terms   301

FOREWORD

The best salespeople ask the best questions.

That makes sense. After all, the better our questions, the better we understand our customers' wants and needs. And the better our suggestions will be, for how we can help them.

And of course, asking questions is much better than the alternative – the horrific 'show up and throw up' approach. We've all seen this – where a salesperson rocks up, and says to the customer: "Sit down, shut up, and watch me tell you when my company was founded. Even better, I'll then show you a map of all our offices"...

So, yes, questions are good. But there are two problems with them:

- Our customers don't know what they don't know. So, our questions will only uncover what's already in their heads; and;
- *We* don't know what we don't know. So, we don't know their desired future, their potential, and how we can best help them achieve it.

Traditional sales approaches don't work

So, is great selling just asking great questions?

No.

Banging out a list of questions that you always ask won't work. It's boring for the customer – nobody wants to be asked "what keeps you awake at night?" for the fifth time that day.

But also these questions only uncover what customers already know.

But what about the stuff you and they don't know you don't know?

Which is why *The Transformational Seller* is such an essential guide for the modern salesperson. Because it takes you step-by-step through everything you need to master, to have these amazing customer conversations – ones that ensure you both discover things you didn't know you didn't know…

… such that you're able to jointly create a solution which delights you both. One that gives them a huge return on invest-ment. And also ensures you feel you've secured a great price.

But why buy this book? And why now?

I mentioned earlier that people have wants and needs.

Well, if you're someone who *wants* to sell more, this book is a must-have. I guarantee you'll learn new ideas, to help boost sales. The stories and examples will give you new ideas and clarity. For instance, you'll like the one which starts "a man goes into a store wanting to buy a power drill. He walks out with a Kindle".

But sadly, in today's world, you might also *need* this book. As technology, AI, algorithms etc become ever more capable, salespeople need to adapt. The machines are taking over the world! They might take over your world; your job. And, unless you can do something that technology can't ever copy, you're replaceable. Very bleak. But very true. To thrive, we *must* adapt.

Do you need Transformational Selling?

That depends. Here are some self-test questions:

- Are you and/or your customers frequently surprised by what they choose to buy?
- How often do you attend sales meetings where both you and the customer learn something *new*?
- How often do customers stop you mid-conversation and say "I've never thought about it like that before" or "I've never heard that – that is useful"?
- What percentage of your deals result in both (1) the customer being delighted by their return on investment, *and* (2) you being delighted by the price?
- If you grade yourself A, B or C for how much you and your customers value your sales interactions, would you both get A+?
- Does every sales interaction achieve the magical 2Ds – (1) do both of you have something to **DO**, and (2) you've also agreed a **DATE** when you'll meet again?

Food for thought?

Many people think sales is hard. And/or that it's about to get harder.

But actually, when you master the techniques in this book, it becomes a lot easier.

You'll have new skills and confidence to help you and customers discover new things – things you didn't know you didn't know.

You'll be better able to do things others can't. That technology can't.

But most importantly, you'll be better able to do something that you and your customers see immense value from.

And when that happens, your sales *will* increase. It's inevitable.

Andy Bounds
Global sales expert – award-winning sales consultant and
best-selling author
andy@andybounds.com

ABOUT THE AUTHORS

Bryn Thompson is a highly experienced sales director, sales trainer and sales recruiter. In a sales career that has spanned over 35 years, he has delivered exceptional sales results, built high performing sales teams and interviewed, placed and trained thousands of sales people and sales leaders. He is a winner of the Sales Leader of the Year Award at the BESMAs (British Excellence in Sales and Marketing Awards).

Bryn created and led the Managed Services team at Pareto for over a decade, specialising in sales and sales leadership training, helping the organisation grow organically from £8m to over £30m turnover. He took their proposition internationally, gaining contracts and subsequently training sellers from across Europe and North America.

He is a fanatical sports person: playing cricket for his local village team and also for Cheshire Seniors, and is a former county rugby player. He plays golf and his handicap is that he's not very good.

Steve Lowndes has spent 25 years as a seller and sales trainer with clients in almost every business-to-business vertical sector across the UK, Europe and North America. He has consulted and advised senior leaders within both large corporate and SMEs, enabling them to deliver exceptional sales results. He is a previous finalist for the BESMA Sales Trainer of the Year Award.

For Steve, a background in science drives a curiosity for breaking down and analysing the sales process. His practical skills are supported by an MBA and a post-graduate diploma in learning and development.

Steve has always been a keen sportsman. Having had to retire from playing rugby, cricket and football on the advice of medical professionals (and just about everyone who saw him play), he now keeps fit through running and cycling with a local club.

Bryn and Steve are co-directors of New World Selling where they put their theories into practice, providing sales teams with the development they need to navigate selling in the New World. If you would like to find out more about their work, please visit their website: **www.newworldselling.co.uk**. If you would like to get in touch you can do via the contacts page on the website.

INTRODUCTION

It's not the strongest of the species that survives, nor the most intelligent, but the one that is most adaptable to change.

Charles Darwin

A DECADE IN THE MAKING

Around ten years ago, the idea of writing this book was conceived over a couple of beers in a bar in Dallas. By that point, we had been colleagues for around 18 months. However, this marked the first time that we had seriously discussed and debated the world of sales.

Although we had come from different backgrounds, collectively we had recruited, trained and assessed thousands of sellers and researched many texts and articles on the subject. We had one key observation in common: despite the wealth of material available, there was an obvious gap in skills and craft across the profession.

We speculated on the reasons for this:

- There are no barriers to entry or formal qualifications needed for a career in sales.
- Very few companies seriously invest in sales development or training.
- Companies tend to recruit sales people based on industry or product knowledge rather than identifiable and transferrable skills.
- The best sellers often get promoted to sales managers/directors without being given the skills to coach and develop others.

The net result is a profession where people are often self-taught and operating on instinct rather than spending time developing and honing their skills.

Since then, we have often discussed the changing world of sales, developed ideas, tested them out and let them grow. As a result, the book we have now written is significantly different from the one we planned a decade ago.

We make frequent reference in this book to the 'New World' which is a term to reflect where we believe business-to-business (B2B) sales is right now and how it is continuing to change, prompting the need for sellers to adapt. The time is ripe to re-evaluate the approach to selling.

This book gives you a step-by-step guide as to how you can achieve this throughout the sales process, how you can truly leverage your expertise in a way that differentiates you from the competition and enables you, and the way that you sell, to become an integral part of the Value Proposition.

THE EVOLUTION OF SALES

Darwin's theory of evolution centres on the idea that species evolve to survive and thrive in different environments. The snow leopard in Asia has evolved to be different from the one that prowls the African savannah. That doesn't mean that the Asian snow leopard's features are superior to its African cousin; its differing features have enabled it to survive the harsh conditions of the Himalayas and those features would be less suited to the hotter plains of the Serengeti. Drop either animal into the other's environment and the chances of survival will be limited.

In the same way, the process and approaches to selling need to evolve and adapt to changing economic and business environments. What may have been successful in the past in one environment is not necessarily going to be successful in the future. The way that sellers adapt will be critical to their own and their companies' success, or even their survival!

As business evolves, so new theories around sales best practice emerge. Dale Carnegie's *How to Win Friends and Influence People* was one of the first texts to regard sales (or at least the ability to influence) as a set of skills and a process. Although written in 1936 and despite the stories being 'of their time', many of the concepts within the book are still relevant today.

Since then, further advancements in sales methodologies have been developed and marketed: Solution Selling; Strategic Selling; SPIN Selling and, more recently, The Challenger Sale. These methodologies all have strong merits. They are built on ideas, research and observation of sellers which enables them to identify the techniques that deliver the most success in the sales arena. Even *The Challenger Sale* (2009), which seemed quite revolutionary with its provocative language, builds on ideas and concepts that we have seen evolving in line with our own experiences and observations.

The main change we have witnessed in B2B selling is the shift from 'products' to 'services' with the rise of subscription models. The expansion of streaming services such as Netflix and Spotify mean that customers no longer buy films or music. Increasingly, they lease vehicles rather than buying them and they can now subscribe to services that allow them to borrow vehicles on demand. In the business world, we have seen the rise of Software as a Service (SaaS) and subsequently Infrastructure as a Service (IaaS) and Platform as a Service (PaaS) which with increased outsourcing have challenged the traditional sales paradigm of the 'transfer of ownership in return for cash'.

Subscription, rather than ownership, is far less tying for organisations and when combined with a sliding scale, dependent upon usage or results, it becomes a flexible and far less risky proposition for the customer. However, selling organisations need to balance these lower barriers to sales with the longer-term problem of customer churn. The lower the commitment required up front, the lower the inclination for adoption or usage and the lower the barriers to switching suppliers. Selling organisations need to be wary of taking a short-term view and they need to think about building customer retention from the outset.

The increasing speed of technological advancement makes it difficult for customers to know what they want or need. Hence, for many customers the sales process needs to focus on a more educational approach to move them away from simply asking for a 'faster horse'.

If I'd asked my customers what they needed, they'd have asked for a faster horse!

This quote is often incorrectly attributed to Henry Ford and we think it illustrates the point neatly.

As organisations offer larger and more complex solutions that cut across multiple business areas, so purchasing decisions rely on broader and more diverse groups of stakeholders, often with centralised procurement functions to oversee the process. Sellers now increasingly need to be able to work with a greater variety of individuals and therefore talk technically *and* strategically.

The idea that you can simply turn up to a meeting with a single customer, ask some questions, pitch your product and then close a sale, all in the space of an hour, is now complete folly for most business propositions.

As these changes have occurred, so sales best practice has needed to evolve from basic Transactional Selling to a more sophisticated Consultative Selling Approach. (Although in practice the successful adoption of Consultative Selling, which has been the predominant sales paradigm for many years, has been extremely mixed.)

THE FUTURE FOR SALES PEOPLE

Can a machine sell better than a human?

Imagine you are looking to buy a new home. You log on to an estate agent's website where you are introduced to 'Sarah' who asks some questions. She shows you several properties and you provide her with feedback on what you like and dislike and are then shown some more.

Having honed in on a particular property, you take a virtual tour and Sarah acts as your guide, highlighting the main features, specifically the ones that are likely to be of most interest to you based on the information she has gleaned. You provide feedback and are asked if you would like to view the property in person.

You arrange a physical viewing and although Sarah isn't there in person, she guides you around remotely, assisting you through the app on your smartphone, answering any questions.

You decide to make an offer on the house. At this point, Sarah will speak to the vendors and, using what she has discovered about you so far, will provide them with advice as to whether or not to accept the offer, the likelihood of you improving it and the probability of a better offer coming in from elsewhere within a given time period. But Sarah doesn't exist – she's AI software.

The advantage of Sarah is that you don't have to pay her a salary or bonus. She works all hours without needing constant motivation or people management skills. She can conduct sales and viewings with multiple customers simultaneously and you don't have to provide her with training; she learns and continues to learn and gets better with every interaction.

The real advantage for the estate agency in 'employing' Sarah is that if the business takes off and the property market booms, they don't have to recruit and train more agents. Conversely, if the market drops, they do not need to downsize their workforce.

As technology advances and the use of artificial intelligence (AI) becomes increasingly prevalent, relatively straightforward sales (those which we refer to as Transactional Sales or the simpler, Consultative Sales) will have little need for the expensive human element. Letting the technology manage the sales process from lead through to order provides consistent and improving results at lower cost, benefitting both the selling and buying organisations.

The selling organisation further benefits from a flexible 'sales force' that can instantaneously scale up and down and doesn't need the same time-consuming people management, equipment such as a laptop and a car and an expense account. Instead, technology can problem solve with an unlimited number of customers simultaneously and can be programmed not to jump in and start pitching too soon unlike far too many sellers we have witnessed!

Sales roles that will still be important in the New World will operate at the higher end of the spectrum, focusing on building highly collaborative relationships. Sellers will need to act as catalysts for change. Here, rather than replacing the human element, technology will augment sales capability, providing predictions and assistance with forecasting. Therefore, sellers will need to use their judgement as to how to respond to the new intelligence at their disposal.

As businesses look to operate in a much leaner way, focusing on their core areas and enabling them to pivot whenever necessary, they will become more reliant on expertise from third-party providers. Sellers will need to demonstrate their expertise and collaborative skills throughout the sales process as if it were an audition for the right to build an equitable relationship with the customer. Arguably, it's this expertise that becomes the most important part of the value proposition.

The distinction between sales and account management will become blurred as the skills, approach and mindset all start to merge. New business sales, focusing on client acquisition, will require a longer-term approach to customer relationships;

working with them to achieve outcomes which have traditionally been aligned to the skill sets currently associated with Customer Success or Account Management teams.

In the same way, excellent account management will require proactive and regular identification of customer needs. Account managers will need to know how to build new value propositions: the very same skills that have traditionally been associated with new business development.

The need for businesses to collaborate for mutual benefit and to secure each other's future will become imperative, and 'early adopter' suppliers will begin to steal a march on their competitors who continue to act in the traditional 'supplier–buyer' way. Mutual survival and growth will be far more dependent on this type of collaboration, where each party develops a much better understanding of what they can offer the other.

Collaboration between suppliers and buyers has never been more important. Suppliers have a strong understanding of how their product or service may benefit a client, but often lack inside knowledge of each client's specific situation. Buyers have a good understanding of their own business but don't always have knowledge of everything that is available, or even how products or services could be adapted to suit their needs.

Issues that arise will be dealt with in a more constructive way when companies see their relationships as collaborative as opposed to having a 'supplier-buyer' mentality. This more collaborative relationship and sharper focus on outcomes will be reflected in the commercial partnerships between suppliers and customers. As we see a continued shift from 'ownership in return for cash' to subscription-based models, we predict a further advancement in collaboration where suppliers will be rewarded for their *results* rather than simply their product, service or activity.

If the outcome is to deliver operational efficiency or increased revenue, then the supplier's remuneration will be reflected in the extent to which these are achieved. No longer will it be good enough to simply supply and then leave the customer to it. Sellers will need to work with their customers to drive implementation and successful adoption.

The focus for both parties will be the achievement of outcomes and for many sellers this represents a major horizon shift. The end game will no longer be the point where the contract is signed or the invoice is paid, it will be when the business outcomes are achieved. The next step in the evolution of sales will see the advent of sellers who **Focus on Outcomes, Leverage Expertise** and **Foster Collaboration** with their customers.

The business stage looks very different now to how it looked ten years ago. The time is ripe for the rise of Transformational Selling: enter, the Transformational Seller.

CHAPTER 1
THE EMERGENCE OF THE TRANSFORMATIONAL SELLER

Change is inevitable, but transformation is by conscious choice

Heather Ash Amara

Transformational Selling defined

Imagine the following scenario:

A man goes into a store wanting to buy a power drill. He walks out with a Kindle.

That's Transformational Selling!

It's not about selling the customer something they don't want or need, it is about examining these needs and finding a solution that delivers the outcome that they are looking for.

"I'm after a drill," the man announces to the store owner as he enters the store

"What sort of drill are you looking for?" asks the storeowner.

"One that's reasonably powerful – I need to be able to drill through solid brick walls."

"OK," responds the storeowner. "So why are you looking to drill through solid brick walls?"

"I need to put some shelves up in my living room," the man explains.

"So, you're a bit of a DIY enthusiast, are you?"

"Goodness, no, I hate DIY. I'd much rather be reading a good book."

"Are you an avid reader then?" the storeowner asks.

"I read whenever I can: at home, on the bus to work, during my lunch hour or on my way home."

What sort of books do you read?"

"Everything: crime, thrillers, comedy, biographies. I love them all. That's the reason why I need the shelves. My bookcase is already full and I need somewhere to store more books."

"And you always carry a book around with you?" the storeowner asks.

"Sometimes more than one – I always want to make sure that if I finish one, I have another ready to start."

"You don't ever like to be without a book to read then, wherever you are, and you don't have enough room to store them. What will happen when these shelves are full?"

"I guess I'll have to put more up," the man ponders.

"So, more DIY? It sounds like you don't really want a drill at all. What you need is a more convenient way of storing books whilst also having a way of accessing any of your books wherever you are."

"That would be perfect!" the man exclaimed.

"I have just the thing…"

The term 'Transformational Selling' was coined around five years ago by one of our clients. It described perfectly the new sales approach that was emerging at that time. This client felt that they needed to find a way to avoid endless time-consuming tender processes that resulted in a race to the bottom. In other words, a race to provide a 'faster horse' at the cheapest possible price.

They recognised that the key to growth and profitability was to explore not what the customer stated that they wanted, but the overall outcomes that the customer needed to achieve. They worked out that their expertise in emergent technology and the 'art of the possible' was perhaps their greatest differentiator and selling point. They saw the value of collaboration. If the customer was interested in a destination rather than the vehicle, then the customer relationship was one worth pursuing. If they were only ever going to be interested in a four-legged mode of transport, then there was little benefit to be had by investing large amounts of time, effort and resource into winning that deal.

Whilst over the last couple of decades huge focus has been placed on adopting consultative behaviours, many organisations by their own admission are still struggling to instil them. This is the most common request for help that we get from business leaders: "My sales team need to be more consultative."

However, with increased complexity of offerings and solutions, the challenge with the consultative approach is the inherent assumption that the *customer knows what their problems are and what they need to do to solve them.*

Here, a heavy burden is placed on the customer's ability to scrutinise every aspect of their business and possess full knowledge regarding the possible options. Customers don't always know what's possible or what's available.

We need a more advanced form of Consultative Selling: a 'Super-Consultative' approach. We refer to this approach as Transformational Selling. We predict that this will become the dominant sales approach in the 'New World'. So, whilst many sales organisations are still playing catch-up from the last evolution, sales practice has already moved on.

One of the great paradoxes of the information age is that customers have never been both better and worse informed. The trouble this provides for sellers is that they often come across customers who know what they need, or more precisely, *think* they know what they need. The old adage used to be: "the customer is always right!"

In the New World this is different. Here we say: "The customer is right about the ultimate outcomes that they want to achieve, everything else needs to be explored!"

Transformational Selling is an approach to sales that is built on the following three pillars:

- **Focus on Outcomes** – to get the customer what they really need.
- **Leverage Expertise** – to understand how best to help the customer to achieve their outcomes.
- **Foster Collaboration** – to guide the customer through their buying journey and beyond.

Figure 1.1: Transformational Selling Model

THE THREE PILLARS OF TRANSFORMATIONAL SELLING

Focus on Outcomes

The Transformational Seller is always focused on outcomes, starting with the question: "What is my customer looking to achieve?" This isn't necessarily what their challenges are, which comes later, but the end result for the customer.

For example, a business owner may be focused on increasing profitability. Alternatively, they may be more concerned with expanding their revenue streams or customer base to make their business more attractive to potential buyers.

Perhaps their goal is to make the business self-sufficient, to provide themselves with an income so that they can take a step back and spend more time on their leisure pursuits. Or they may have a vision aligned to altruism or providing benefits for the wider society.

Other decision makers in organisations will have different goals, objectives, key performance indicators (KPIs) and targets. These may unlock extrinsic rewards such as bonuses, pay rises or promotions; or drive intrinsic benefits such as personal growth, recognition, status and achievement. It's easy for sellers to overlook the significance of *intrinsic* motivations and the emotional drivers of customers.

The focus for the Transformational Seller is on establishing the business or professional goals for individual stakeholders and the business overall, and work towards how their offering can help to achieve these collectively.

Leverage Expertise

The more you understand your customer's outcomes, the better you can guide them to what they actually need. All too often, customers have pre-conceived ideas. Whilst they may be on the right lines, they are not usually experts in your products, services or industry. They don't necessarily understand what is available and therefore end up asking for the proverbial 'faster horse'.

The role of the Transformational Seller is not just to listen and respond to what the customer asks for, but to explore the ultimate results they wish to achieve and the potential barriers, before making appropriate recommendations.

The Transformational Seller acts as any other professional advisor. Accountants or lawyers don't simply do what their clients ask them to: they explore, develop strategies, and highlight the risks and benefits of various options before advising on the best course of action. Similarly, a doctor analyses a patient's symptoms and prescribes the best course of treatment. They don't just prescribe a course of drugs because the patient asked for them (or at least they shouldn't!).

If you are relatively new to sales or your industry, it can appear challenging to leverage the expertise that you don't yet feel you possess. However, we've heard it said that as long as you know one percent more than the other party, you can be considered the expert. This may sound cynical but there are always areas where you know more than your customer, no matter how new you are to an industry. This will increase with time and experience.

These areas should go beyond your own products and services, and onto how these solve problems for customers, the typical issues that they face, what prevents them from achieving their outcomes and how other customers have resolved such issues.

In your first few weeks within an organisation, it's these areas that you should determine to enable you to start having meaningful conversations with customers.

Foster Collaboration

Too many sellers develop customer relationships which can be described as having a master–servant dynamic. The Transformational Seller must enter into a relationship on an equal footing if they are to encourage the customer to share information around their targets, measures for success, and current performance metrics, in addition to the longer-term goals and strategies of the business.

Sellers also need to explore potential weaknesses and failings within the customer's current arrangements to fully understand and diagnose what is getting in the way of their desired outcomes. They need to redefine their customer's needs and requirements and help them to navigate their way through their buying journey, engage with other contacts or sponsors and work through the complexities of the decision-making process.

A key to collaboration is the Transformational Seller's horizon, best exemplified by the question: "When is the sale complete?"

A Transactional Seller may say this is when the customer signs the contract (or perhaps when they pay the invoice). A Consultative Seller might suggest that it's when the product or service is installed, and the problem has been fixed.

The Transformational Seller has a different mindset: the deal is only complete once the customer has achieved their outcomes, by which time they will then be collaborating on how to achieve the next outcome.

THE CONDITIONS FOR TRANSFORMATIONAL SELLING

There is an inherent assumption that 'best practice' in sales is always the same, whatever the industry or whichever product or service you are selling.

Consider the TV show *The Apprentice* when the candidates are set a selling task, often involving a relatively low value, impulse or commodity item targeted at members of the public. Those who succeed in making the most sales use this as evidence as to their suitability to achieve the ultimate prize: running their own business with Lord Sugar's backing and selling more complex and higher value solutions.

The reality is that selling burgers in the street and complex software solutions to major corporations requires a vastly different selling approach. The fancy sales patter that encourages a hungry shopper to pay £4 for a burger will not seduce the CEO of a multinational corporation to part with £4m for an Enterprise Software Solution.

However, the success of these candidates to complete such transactional trades provides some pointers to overall sales success. This isn't because they demonstrate transferrable skills sets. Rather, they evidence their hunger and desire to succeed, which is every bit as important (possibly even more so).

While analysing various sales approaches over the years, we have seen different prevailing conditions that dictate the required approach. These range from the complexity of the solution, the degree of commoditisation, the level of risk and effort for the customer to implement the solution and the customer's own understanding and awareness of the need for a solution. We have captured these in the *Seven Conditions for Selling Model.*

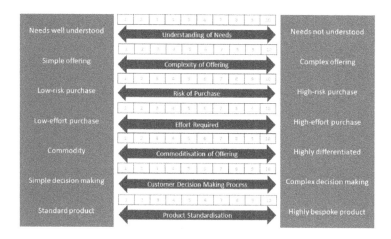

Figure 1.2: 'The 7 Conditions for Selling'

The conditions that influence the mode of selling are based upon:

Understanding Needs – the extent to which the customer understands their needs, and the options and solutions available to them.

Complexity – the requirement to tailor products or services, the number of stakeholders involved in the process and the degree of integration or change required.

Risk – the scale of investment or the changes required as a result of the purchase. Customer perception of risk is one of the main reasons that larger sales opportunities fall through, as companies opt to play it safe and continue operating in the same way, however inefficient or ineffective that may be.

Effort – the implications and work involved in implementing a solution: physical installation or integration into existing systems; adoption of a different way of working; and new routines or working practices to be implemented. Training staff is often an issue as is the potential impact on productivity whilst they are learning and adjusting.

Commoditisation – the degree to which products and services are commoditised or differentiated. The customer perception of the offering as a commodity often leads to: driving the process transactionally; shortcutting the Discovery Phase; focusing on availability and price; or requesting literature and proposals without engaging directly with the supplier. Formal buying processes such as requests for proposals (RFPs) and tenders often have this effect.

Defining 'Commoditisation'

We use this term to describe products or services for which there is, in the customer's mind at least, little or no discernible difference between suppliers and competitors. As such, the customer's purchasing decision is heavily weighted on price and availability.

Diversity of the Decision-Making Unit – the idea of a single 'decision maker' is becoming outmoded in B2B sales. Decisions are now generally made by groups comprising disparate persons and departments, referred to as the Decision-Making Unit (DMU). The use of the word 'unit' is something of a misnomer as these opinions are rarely unified, with varying perspectives on what a good provider or solution looks like.

Standardisation – the extent to which the offering is standard (i.e., out of the box) or is tailored or built from scratch for the customer. Bespoke or tailored offerings tend to have increased complexity and require customer and seller to work more closely together.

Exercise: Find your place on the Transactional to Transformational Spectrum

Review your own sales offering and market conditions and assign a score to each of the seven conditions from 1–10. If the scores are mostly low, then the Transactional Approach is likely to be the most dominant and effective form of selling. Higher scores (above 50) dictate the need to develop a more Transformational Approach.

Note that those sales conditions that tend towards the Transactional and lower end Consultative are increasingly being replaced by automation in the New World.

Avoiding Seller Extinction – The Left to Right Shift

The degree to which your sales attributes align with these conditions will reflect the natural place that you should be looking to occupy on the spectrum in Figure 1.3.

Figure 1.3: The Transactional to Transformational Spectrum

Note of caution, particularly in the B2B world, these conditions have changed and will require movement by the seller from left to right.

Many sellers operate too far to the left of the ideal position on the spectrum, demonstrating Transactional behaviours where the conditions suggest a more Consultative or Transformational Approach.

In the New World, the left-hand side of the spectrum will increasingly be occupied by e-commerce and technological innovation. To avoid becoming a victim of this, many sellers will need to start changing their behaviours.

The next chapter will delve more deeply into what those behaviours should look like and how sellers can work in tandem with clients in a more transformational capacity. However, those sellers who continue to operate to the left of this spectrum, either by default or design, will either fade away or be replaced by less expensive means.

CHAPTER SUMMARY

- Transformational Selling is based on three core pillars: **Focus on Outcomes**, **Leverage Expertise** and **Foster Collaboration**.
- To **Focus on Outcomes** involves exploring the customer's ultimate goals, targets and objectives and aligning your offering towards the achievement of these.
- To **Leverage Expertise**, the Transformational Seller uses expertise gained from previous customer experiences to guide the customer towards the solutions that will best achieve their desired outcomes. They will consider the challenges and issues that might derail their progress.
- To **Foster Collaboration**, the Transformational Seller looks beyond the horizon of the contract being signed, the product being implemented, or the invoice being

paid, and views the sale as only being complete when the customer has achieved their stated outcomes.

- The seven conditions that lend themselves towards adopting a transformational approach are: the customer's understanding of their needs; the complexity of the solution; the degree of risk; the effort required to implement the solution; the degree of differentiation versus commoditisation; the diversity of the DMU; and the level of standardisation versus bespoke solutions.
- There's a spectrum of approaches from Transactional to Transformational and the optimal place on the spectrum is dictated by the seven conditions outlined.
- Our experience indicates there is a very strong tendency for sellers to operate too far to the left of the optimal position on the spectrum.
- In the New World, sellers operating to the left will increasingly be replaced by technology and only the Transformational Seller will ultimately survive and thrive.

CHAPTER 2
THE BEHAVIOURS OF THE TRANSFORMATIONAL SELLER

A cynic is a man who knows the price of everything and the value of nothing.

Oscar Wilde

"My customers don't like being sold to."

We've heard that statement many times from sellers we term 'reluctant sellers'. These are those who are in denial as to what their role really is. They may be one of the following:

- Professional advisers/experts in their field – required to generate their own work or 'kill what they eat'.
- Account managers – see their role as delivering a great customer experience and only servicing their customer's existing business.

- Sellers – believe in waiting for their customer to buy (i.e., the 'order-takers').

This statement protects such sellers from going outside of their comfort zones and presents a tainted view of sales. Our answer is simply: "If your customers don't like being sold to, then you're doing something wrong!"

In Chapter, 1 we explored the seven conditions that lend themselves to adopting a Transformational Approach and then we started to identify how the Transformational Seller goes about their trade.

The ideal position to be on the Transactional to Transformational Spectrum will depend upon the conditions that you operate under and will often vary for different customers and the key elements of your offering. Your approach will need to be flexible. A major 'enterprise' sale, for example, may sit in a very different place on the spectrum to a component or consumable sale to the same customer. It's important that you continually re-evaluate your position on the spectrum.

This chapter explores the behaviours associated with the Transactional, Consultative and Transformational modes of selling, to enable you to identify the modes that should be adopted, and those that need to be left behind as you journey towards becoming a Transformational Seller.

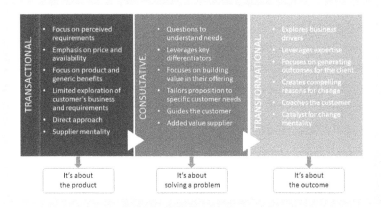

Figure 2.1: Transactional – Consultative – Transformational Behaviours

TRANSACTIONAL BEHAVIOURS

We have seen that the Transactional Approach works where the customer has a good understanding of their requirements: the offering is simple and standardised, there's limited differentiation and there's a low risk or effort for the customer.

We are highlighting Transactional behaviours to sense check the approach that needs to change when making the left to right shift from Transactional to Transformational.

Focus on Perceived Requirements or Expressed Needs

Transactional Selling assumes that customer's wants or needs are interchangeable: if they want it, they must also need it. It also assumes that they have a sound understanding of the problem to be solved and are fully aware of the potential solutions available. It's often an 'order-taking' mentality without any added value from the seller, which therefore makes it easier to replicate through technology and e-commerce.

Emphasis on Price and Availability

With an assumption, made by the customer or seller, that the product or service is relatively commoditised, price and availability become the only levers to engage the customer, create urgency and progress the sale. Being cheaper than the alternatives, together with 'availability' which focuses on either timely delivery ("we can get that to you tomorrow by 9am") or limited availability ("only three rooms still available on these dates"), is one route to securing a customer's commitment.

Product Focused and Generic Benefit Driven

Transactional Seller conversations are dominated by the product. The demonstration or pitch comes early in the sales process with only superficial discovery of customer needs. Information about the product may include generic 'benefits' and case studies, but lack specific links to the problems, challenges or outcomes for each customer and their situation.

Limited Exploration of the Customer's Business and Requirements

The Transactional Seller is typically looking to get to a 'yes' via the shortest route possible. The process is: Qualify – Pitch – Close. Qualification is limited to the practical and technical: can the customer actually buy and use what is being sold?

Direct Approach to Influence

The Transactional Seller aims to deliver a compelling reason for their customer to buy through telling rather than asking. Any resistance from the customer is met with either a logical and pre-prepared statement or often the lowering of the price or by throwing in some extras for a quick sale.

Supplier Mentality

The relationship is often imbalanced in favour of the customer with the supplier being somewhat subservient. The supplier does what they need to do to keep the customer on-side and gives them what they ask for in return for securing an order in the most direct and timely manner possible.

CONSULTATIVE SELLER BEHAVIOURS

As we start to move across the spectrum from left to right, we encounter the Consultative Seller behaviours which are better aligned to organisations offering a differentiated product or service, a more complex or bespoke solution, or a transaction that involves a greater degree of risk or commitment from the customer.

Although the Consultative Approach has been the dominant paradigm within B2B sales over the last forty years, many organisations are still struggling to master it. Those that have, are now better placed to make the requisite shift to Transformational Selling.

The Transformational Seller has evolved from the Consultative Seller and many of the behaviours are built upon those that are embedded within the Consultative Approach.

Questions to Understand Customer's Needs

There is one fundamental differences between the Transactional Seller and the Consultative Seller. The Transactional Seller believes that their customer knows what they need whereas the Consultative Seller is aware that their customer may not necessarily know exactly what they need.

The customer may be aware of a problem or an opportunity to improve, and this forms the basis for discussion. The Consultative Seller's primary aim is to conduct an effective Discovery Phase and, through questioning and listening, gain an understanding of the customer's problems and therefore their requirements.

Defining 'Problem'

We will come up against the word 'problem' frequently in this book as it is fundamental to how and why businesses (and individuals) buy. In essence we are defining a **problem** as anything that could be fixed or improved for the benefit of the business.

It could be something affecting overall performance, such as a piece of equipment that is running slowly or material that is being wasted, or an opportunity that the business is unable to take advantage of due to lack of a resource. It could also be something that represents a potential risk to the business (e.g., a cyber-attack).

Leverages the Key Differentiators

The Consultative Seller recognises the need to ensure that their product or service isn't commoditised by the customer. Commoditisation leads to price discussions, discounting and often a race to the bottom.

Differentiation is therefore essential in creating the drive to switch suppliers or, when purchasing a new product or solution, choosing a more expensive or premium option over cheaper alternatives. The Consultative Seller focuses on their key differentiators and, through a better understanding of their customer's problems, seeks to make the link between how their differences will better alleviate them.

Focuses on Building Value in their Offering

Defining 'Value'

From a Consultative Selling perspective, the notion of value comes from the source of the word itself: for something to have value it must be 'valuable'. Something can be described as valuable because:

- it's scarce or different;
- it solves a problem.

The term **value** is often bandied around alongside the notion of selling on 'value not price'. However, there's often a disconnect between its usage and the origin of its meaning.

For example, when a major UK retailer launched its 'Value Range', these products were cheaper and arguably of lower quality than their standard own-label brand. In this case, the word became synonymous with 'cheap'. In the same way we frequently see value used to describe the least expensive option by both buyers and sellers.

Guides the Customer

A key difference between the Transactional and Consultative Seller is the degree to which each uses their knowledge and expertise within the sales process.

The Transactional Seller is less concerned with analysing customer problems and making recommendations; any advice provided is limited to product options and preferences.

The Consultative Seller will aim to tailor the solution to their customer's needs, question around problems and act as a sounding board for the customer. They will look to provide a solution to the problem that has been identified.

Added-Value Supplier Mentality

As a Value-Added Supplier, the mentality of the Consultative Seller is that price isn't everything. Even though the competition may have a cheaper offering, they focus on winning the deal through demonstrating the **value** of their offering and creating real buy-in to their solution.

The fact is that whilst most companies can't afford to take a 'money is no object' approach to spending, businesses generally appreciate that if the **problem** is significant enough and the difference is clear, then the additional premium is worth paying.

Deals are never lost purely on price. If the customer opts for a cheaper alternative, then it's because the seller didn't build enough value.

Customers don't always buy the cheapest

Steve: We once ran a session for a group of sales managers at an engineering company's annual sales conference. The conference theme was how to become a 'Value Added Supplier'.

The company had a strong value proposition, but their greatest obstacle was the mindset of their sales force, who had been operating in a transactional way for so long they couldn't see beyond the price issue.

In the morning, the CEO had presented findings from industry research demonstrating that price was not the main factor in customers selecting a provider. This was reinforced during a Q&A session with a couple of their key customers who re-emphasised the importance of quality, expertise and reliability when choosing a supplier.

We kicked off an afternoon break-out session with the sales managers focusing back on the value-price conversation. One of the managers spoke up.

"Despite what's been said, the fact is that if the customer can get a cheaper option elsewhere, that's what they will do." There was a general buzz of agreement around the room.

"OK, take look out of the window," we suggested. Outside was the conference centre car park, where most of the attendees had parked. "What do you see?"

They looked out at row after row of premium and prestige vehicles: BMWs, Mercedes, Audis, Jaguars etc.

"Those were chosen by you as your business vehicle and paid for by your company. How many of those were the cheapest option available? So can we agree that businesses don't always take the cheapest option?"

TRANSFORMATIONAL SALES BEHAVIOURS

As we move across the Transactional–Consultative–Transformational Spectrum, the significance of the purchase becomes greater, potential risks increase, the solution becomes more complex, and the needs may be less easily recognised.

We have outlined the three core principles of the Transformational Selling Approach – **Focuses on Outcomes, Leverages Expertise** and **Fosters Collaboration** – and will now explore the behaviours that underpin this approach. These behaviours do not replace those of the Consultative Seller, they add another layer.

Transformational Sellers understand the importance of building value, leveraging differentiators and exploring the customer's problems. They also recognise that they are in a unique position to utilise their expertise and knowledge to enhance both their customer's business and their own sales performance as a result.

Their role is not to just to solve problems, it is to help the customer identify them and provide the solution.

Ultimately, the Transformational Seller is looking to be a **catalyst for change** in terms of the way in which the customer engages with them, the manner in which they make decisions and the way in which they operate.

Explores Business Drivers and Strategies

The Transformational Seller goes beyond simply exploring the customer's operational issues. They move the conversation to a higher level, to understand what success looks like for the customer and what they are trying to achieve: their business outcomes.

Each customer will have their own critical objectives that fit with the wider business strategy. For example, a production manager may be targeted with the overall operational efficiency of the production facility whereas a marketing director may be assigned responsibility for the number of inbound enquiries generated. A sales director is likely to be targeted on the growth in sales, perhaps with an emphasis on new client acquisitions or on selling multiple product lines.

Whatever their objectives, these will be aligned to a broader strategy for the business and are significant not only to the main contact, but also to those they report to (very often the people that will need to be convinced to win the deal). It's this hierarchy of objectives that the Transformational Seller seeks to understand.

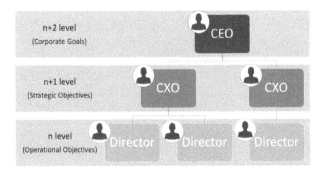

Figure 2.2: Hierarchy of Objectives ('n' being the key contact)

The New World is seeing more complex decision making within businesses and greater risk aversion. It will become increasingly important to sell not only to 'n level' contacts (the main contact) but also n+1 and n+2 levels within an organisation. The reverse is also true. We have seen many organisations who have managed to convince C-Suite and above to purchase, only to find subsequent low adoption of the solution at an operational level – which can be a particular problem for subscription-based sales.

It is therefore not enough to only know about the problems or issues that your initial contact is facing. As a Transformational Seller you need to explore:

- The specific objectives that n (the main contact) is targeted to achieve.
- How these objectives fit with the objectives for n+1, n+2 levels.
- How these align with the overall strategy and / or mission for the organisation.

In understanding all of what we have so far explained, you will be able to establish and articulate how your offering fits in with the overall value chain. You will then ensure that you create a more engaging and compelling argument that can be translated to all levels of the business.

Uses Expertise as a Differentiator

A key attribute of the Transformational Seller is their level of expertise. Even relatively inexperienced sellers can quickly build their expertise. For many sellers this starts with product knowledge which forms the focus for many organisations' sales or onboarding training. However important good product knowledge might be – and its importance can't be stressed strongly enough – it's not simply how they work, but how they support the customer in achieving their desired outcomes that needs to be studied and understood.

Further to this, the Transformational Seller develops expertise through their understanding of the challenges and issues faced by customers and how they have successfully overcome these (not just in reference to their offering but broader strategies as well) together with the pitfalls and mistakes they may have made along the way.

Higher-level expertise takes considerable time to build up. The Transformational Seller recognises that they don't directly have to be the fount of all knowledge. The expertise that they leverage comes through the broader knowledge base of each client organisation they work with and the wealth of experience and ideas that sit within their own company. They gain industry knowledge and awareness of new trends and upcoming changes. They also question to understand the customer's business, key drivers, strategic aims and desired outcomes in relation to industry changes.

Many customers are so busy in the day-to-day management of their business that the chance to come up for air and take a view of what's going on outside their own organisation is a luxury they can ill afford. The ability of the Transformational Seller to identify and disseminate best practice (without betraying specific client confidences) is where they add real value.

Focuses on Generating Outcomes for the Client

Aligned to the idea of understanding the customer's business goals and strategies, the Transformational Seller demonstrates their understanding of where their products and services sit within the value chain.

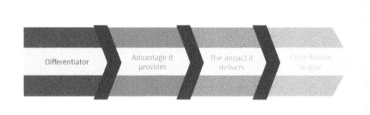

Figure 2.3: Value Chain Linking Differentiators to Outcomes

Throughout the sales process, the Transformational Seller continues to bring the focus, whether through their questioning, pitching, proposal or negotiation, back to the overall outcomes that their customer is looking to achieve.

Value Chain: example

Steve: We worked with a leading supplier of heavy plant equipment who had a premium offering in the market. The brand was well recognised and respected, but this came at a price in an industry where buyers were always looking to drive down costs.

They had several points of differentiation, but sellers continually struggled to persuade a customer to part with an extra £20,000 for a machine that moved earth from one place to another. On paper, it appeared to be exactly the same as their competitors' offerings.

For example, one of their features was air conditioning within the cabins. This was something that few competitors were offering at the time and although customers recognised this as an advantage, it was deemed a 'nice to have' rather than essential.

In order to leverage this, the first link the sellers needed to make was between the comfort of the machine operator and their productivity. In warmer temperatures, cabins became extremely hot and operators needed to take more breaks. They therefore suffered from fatigue faster and as a result their level of productivity diminished. This meant that their output was reduced. This perspective now focused the conversation on solving a problem: how to maintain optimum productivity during warm weather.

The Transformational Seller takes this a step further. The potential loss of productivity needs to link to specific outcomes for the customer rather than generic advantages such as completing the project on time.

The sellers needed to understand more detail regarding their customer's deadlines, the penalty clauses within the contract, the broader reputational consequences of not completing on time and the potential health and safety ramifications.

Once they started opening up these issues, they were able to create the distinct value chain that linked their offering through to the customer's higher-level outcomes.

Figure 2.4: Value Chain for Air-Conditioned Cabs

Creates a Compelling Reason for Change

Change is at the heart of the Transformational Seller's focus. Put simply, this means helping customers make positive purchasing decisions to help achievement of their outcomes.

This is likely to involve helping the customer to change their thinking in the following ways:

- They may need them to think differently about their purchasing decisions and the criteria on which they base their choice (e.g., price, brand, specification).
- The Transformational Seller may need the customer to reconsider the scope of the potential decision they are making. Too often, customers, for simplicity or financial reasons, make short-term decisions that neglect the longer-term results that they are looking for. They swap out a piece of machinery in their production line that is worn out rather than looking at the reasons *why* it has deteriorated and issues that may be occurring up or

down stream. They purchase a piece of office software based on brand but don't consider the changes their people need to make to maximise its potential. They train their sales team in new sales techniques but don't consider developing the skills of their managers and their relative ability to coach or embed these skills.

- The Transformational Seller will almost certainly need to open their customer's eyes to the problems that they didn't recognise they had. Through their expertise, they are able to alert their customer to issues that exist within their current operations, processes and results.

The aim of the Transformational Seller is to create what we refer to as the 'oh s**t' moment – the *key moment* which shifts the client's thinking. This often comes from asking questions that explore the validity of the customer's assumptions and opens up ideas that they hadn't previously considered: the critical point where your customer turns to you and says thoughtfully, "That's a good question."

The difference that a single question can make

Bryn: Shortly after the Brexit vote in 2016, we flew to Paris to pitch for a major training contract. We were up against two French companies. Given that the client and their parent company were both French (and Brexit was not exactly a popular issue there), we felt that the odds were stacked against us.

The tender had been detailed and precise, and we had managed to get shortlisted. However, the stage where we were due to pitch our ideas to the client was to be the first time we had met them. It was the classic procurement-led, arms-length process: answer written questions and then come in to present as part of a 'beauty parade'.

The presentation was going quite well, and the audience of decision makers seemed reasonably engaged, if still a little guarded. Our concern was whether we were different enough from the competition, who had a distinct 'home advantage'. It was time to act. We made the following statement.

"The challenge with ensuring that the training has an impact is on being confident that your front-line managers can coach and embed these skills on a daily basis. Too often though, we find that managers haven't been given the skills they need to be great coaches." We then followed this up with a key question:

"When the training is over, how do you plan to protect your investment?"

Suddenly the dynamic changed. Our question prompted a round table discussion from the group about their sales management team. They talked about how even though most of them had been promoted from being good sellers, few, if any, had any leadership training. We continued to ask questions around their observations and experience. We were no longer talking or presenting and the client was opening up with many concerns they hadn't previously discussed as a group.

This one question was the catalyst to a conversation that led to a substantial six figure contract with increased scope (and order value) for the training of the management team.

Coaches the Customer

In the world of coaching, the professional coach is concerned with change. They aim to help their clients make substantial shifts in behaviours, attitudes, mindset and actions to achieve longer-term goals and outcomes.

Therefore, the role of the Transformational Seller and professional coach are very closely aligned and, not surprisingly, the skills and techniques applied by both should be mirrored. The coach asks the 'why' questions, uncovers assumptions and opens up their client's mind to new possibilities in the same way that the Transformational Seller does.

Despite the obvious overlap, until now very little has been documented around the explicit link between sales and coaching. We will be returning to this idea at numerous stages throughout this book, investigating how the principles from professional coaching can be applied in the seller–customer context.

Collaboration for Change Mentality

The mentality of 'collaboration for change' permeates everything that the Transformational Seller does. They recognise that they potentially have something very valuable to offer, not just in terms of their products and services but also the advice, guidance and expertise that they bring.

They understand that they themselves are a key part of the value proposition, and that over the course of their engagement with the client, what they bring to the conversation lies beyond just their products and services.

They enter into conversations with customers with a view to enabling them to find better ways to achieve their objectives, reflect on what they are doing and identify what is getting in the way of success. They are constantly looking to create those moments with the customer.

The Transformational Seller needs to enter into the engagement on an equal footing and not, as so many sellers do, with a mindset that they are subservient. That doesn't mean they should be arrogant or disrespect what the customer has to say, but it does mean recognising their own worth.

Starting out on the right foot

Andy Bounds, the well-respected sales author and speaker, argues that when meeting with a client, you should never thank them for their time. His assertion is that when you thank them for taking time to meet, you are suggesting that somehow their time is more valuable than yours and that they are doing you a favour by granting an audience.

By starting off a relationship in this way – as an implied 'master and servant' – you make it more difficult to be accepted as an equal, reduce your credibility as an expert and limit the chances of changing the customer's thinking. Andy suggested that thanking customers for their time is often a pre-curser to capitulating on price.

This suggestion has caused consternation amongst some observers who are insistent that good manners were vitally important and that not thanking you customer for their time is somewhat discourteous.

In our view, these observers are missing the point. There is no suggestion in Andy's argument of being rude, or arrogant. Instead, Andy is asking us to think about the language and tone that we use to create and cement a perception that can be hard to change. By opening a conversation with "it's great for us to get some time together" we can acknowledge the value that we place on speaking with the prospect without undermining or belittling our own contribution to the conversation.

In the same way, we see many sellers constantly running around after their customers, producing proposals and quotations, redrafting these and spending hours producing information at their customer's request whilst getting nothing back in return. It's what we term **The Labrador Effect,** on the basis that a Labrador will always fetch the slipper regardless of the reward on offer.

We will examine the concept of reciprocity and active commitment in Chapter 14. For now it's important to recognise that as a Transformational Seller you value your own time and expertise. If you don't value it, you can't expect your customer to.

BECOMING TRANSFORMATIONAL – MAKING THE SHIFT FROM LEFT TO RIGHT

Commoditisation is a challenge; particularly where relatively standard products lack the complexity to be tailored to customer needs. Even where product differentiation is limited, we have worked with companies who have already recognised the limited future in continuing to operate in a Transactional way. They are committed to avoiding the 'commodity trap'.

Moving across the TCT Spectrum

Steve: We worked with a wholesale distributor of metals (steel and aluminium sheets, rods and extrusions). Metal is a good example of a purely commoditised product. When the customer needed to buy, there were only two criteria that really mattered: the speed of delivery and price.

The sellers had always relied on rapport and good relationships to be their differentiator but recognised in tougher economic times these weren't going to cut it. They needed to find creative ways of differentiating themselves and their offering and a unique way of selling their products.

The starting point came through one simple addition to their sales process. They started asking 'why?' This opened up conversations exploring what their customer was manufacturing, their timescales, the other materials they were using, their challenges and issues. As a result, instead of just talking about price, the sellers started collaborating with the customer on issues such as stock control, future requirements, advice on alternative materials, just-in-time delivery and the reduction of wastage and off-cuts.

Suddenly the price per kilo seemed a lot less important.

We have also worked with a client supplying workflow software to businesses to help manage a large volume of client requests. Their target market is companies with large customer bases, typically in the areas of financial services, utilities and telecoms.

They had an impressive offering which matched many of the conditions at the Transformational end of the spectrum. At the start of the engagement, we were invited to speak at their annual conference where we also got to hear from some of their customers. One recently acquired customer got up to speak and announced:

"We were sold this product on the basis that it could save us considerable amounts of time and money; that we could do the same amount of work with only half the staff and that it would speed up response times. Whilst that seemed appealing, the idea of letting half our employees go would be difficult for the business to accept and is counter-intuitive to many of our values.

"However, we realised that by implementing this system, which would free up staff time, it would create the opportunity to launch new and more complex products to our customers. These were to be products that would otherwise be prohibitively difficult to introduce and service. This system would enable us to innovate and stay ahead of our competitors, increase customer retention as well as acquire thousands of new customers.

"It was sold to us as a way of reducing operating costs, but what we realised is that we now had something that can help drive our business forward and cement our position in the market."

This example we have given demonstrates the difference between the Consultative and Transformational approaches. Whilst in this case the sale happened, this was down to the customer having recognised the potential for themselves not necessarily down to the skills and approach of the seller.

The Consultative Seller focuses on the customer's problem (which is labour intensive and costly in terms of administration) and looks to solve it. The Transformational Seller understands their customer's outcomes, opens the customer's eyes to the possibilities and let's their expertise and know-how be the compelling point of difference.

We will work on these ideas throughout the book by looking at specific tools and techniques that can be introduced simply and easily into your sales approach. We aim to take you several steps along the path on your left-to-right journey. Whilst these skills are vital, the greatest challenge to making that shift is adopting the right mindset and attitude. Becoming Transformational is not easy and without the willingness to abandon your comfort zone, many sellers will struggle.

As we see from these examples, the role of the seller will not be to transact with the customer simply to give them what they asked for in most efficient way possible. Instead, sellers will need to guide and facilitate the customer through the complexities of understanding what they really need and how best to achieve their desired outcomes.

The next chapter looks at the complex journey that the customer goes through when making a purchasing decision and the approach the Transformational Seller takes in guiding them on that journey.

Exercise: Creating Value Chains

Creating value chains is a key way to link the difference in your offering with the outcomes that your customer is looking to achieve from both an operational and a strategic perspective. As a starting point you should consider the following questions:

1. What are the typical outcomes or objectives your customers are trying to achieve from an operational perspective?
2. How do these objectives fit in with the broader, more strategic objectives of each customer's organisation?
3. How do the specific aspects of your offering enable your customers to achieve these operational and ultimately strategic objectives?

Next make the links between the specific aspects that you identified in Step 3 and the Outcomes/Objectives you identified in Steps 1 and 2, to create a series of value chains. (There are examples earlier in the chapter.)

If it helps, consider a specific sales opportunity you are working on right now.

CHAPTER SUMMARY

- The Transactional Approach is still observable today within the B2B sales arena, often by mistake rather than design. However, the long-term future for the Transactional Seller is limited and, sellers and sales leaders alike need to develop and evolve their approach or risk being phased out in the near future.
- The Consultative Approach has been the major paradigm for B2B sales for many years. Its focus has been on identifying and solving customer problems and whilst this provides a foundation for Transformational Selling, sellers will need to adapt and develop their skill sets further if they are to remain successful and relevant.
- The Transformational Approach, with its focus on outcomes, expertise and collaboration is where the future of B2B sales lies. The ability to help customers identify the issues they didn't know that they had (or will have) and collaborate on implementing the

solution or mitigation for these, whilst focusing on their short and long-term goals will not only drive sales success but ensure that technology supports rather than replaces them.

- All B2B sellers need to re-evaluate their position on the TCT Spectrum, identify ways in which they can take a step to the right and avoid the natural drift to the left that we see all too often.

CHAPTER 3
THE CUSTOMER BUYING JOURNEY

People don't buy for logical reasons. They buy for emotional reasons.

Zig Ziglar

The customer buying journey – our 'moment'

Steve: An epiphany, or, 'oh s**t' moment came almost 20 years ago when we were creating a training programme supporting a 1,500-strong sales force in shifting to what was referred to then, coincidentally, as the 'New World'. In effect, we were attempting to move the sales force from left to right, away from the typical Transactional Approach that was prevalent in their business at the time.

Their Head of Sales was happy with the content of the programme, but felt it needed something else to bring it to life. He suggested it be accompanied by a video that would support and reinforce the key messages.

Back when the internet was relatively new and TED talks were unheard of, training videos were a vital source of visual support for many development initiatives. The concept of storytelling to support key messages was well founded and we agreed it could add to the programme, if only we could find a suitable one. Most videos we had seen were very basic and therefore unlikely to convey the messaging required, and, for want of a better word, were a bit 'naff'.

We visited a company that specialised in training films and spent a day working through their catalogue, much of which we discounted very quickly. The videos were either too basic or cheesy. They failed to deliver anything close to the message we wanted.

Most of the videos followed a similar format: an inexperienced but enthusiastic seller and a wise mentor guiding them through the errors being made at each stage of the sales process. It was akin to Bill Murray in *Groundhog Day* – learning from their mistakes to enable them to progress to the next stage of the sale.

We were losing hope when we stumbled across one that, if perhaps a little contrived, stood out. It supported the key messages that we were trying to deliver and although we'd have liked it to provide more detail around the 'how', it was somehow different from all the others.

What was it that made this video stand out? It soon became apparent. This was the only sales video where the central character was the **customer** and not the seller. The narrative came from the customer's perspective not the supplier's.

This lightbulb moment cemented an idea that we had been nurturing for some time – that great selling is not about taking your customer through your sales process; it's about guiding and facilitating your customer around their buying journey.

THE CUSTOMER BUYING JOURNEY

Organisations invest a great deal of time in developing and monitoring their sales processes which, in theory, enables them to manage and control sales activity more effectively. The challenge is that these sales processes are almost always developed and documented from the organisation's perspective.

Such processes require updates as to whether sellers have delivered a proposal, conducted a demonstration or a proof of concept, and the level of qualification completed. Whilst there is nothing inherently wrong with all of this, the piece that is missing is that whilst they may be going through a sales process, the customer is going through their own buying journey.

The Transformational Seller is guided by a set of behaviours and a mindset and recognises that their role is to collaborate with their customer, and to assist them through the buying journey towards the achievement of their desired outcomes.

Therefore, the emphasis should be far less on where you are in the sales process and more on where your customer is. Sales opportunities typically fall down when the sales process and the buying journey are out of sync.

There are six key stages to the customer's buying journey and although these are presented as a logical linear sequence it is worth noting that:

- Some of these stages are iterative and customers go back and forth between different stages.
- The 'customer' may be a group of stakeholders who may not all go through this journey at the same pace.
- In order to understand the journey well, you need to be able to influence it.

As we all have experience of being customers, we should be able to empathise with our customers as they go through their buying journey.

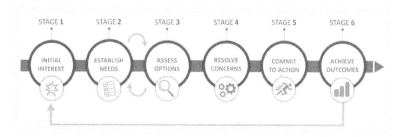

Figure 3.1: The Six Stages of the Customer Buying Journey

STAGE 1 – INITIAL INTEREST

Purchasing a complex product or service or one carrying a significant degree of risk is not something businesses enter into lightly, and this is coming under much greater scrutiny in the New World.

The issue of getting a customer's time to open up discussions is a challenge that sales development representatives know only too well. People tend to be resistant to change and are inherently risk averse. The reasons behind this may lie in the evolutionary journey of the human race, where avoiding risk began as a survival mechanism. What we can be sure about is our preference for certainty even if it means we end up with an average result. We don't like taking the risk even if there is a chance of a better outcome.

This thinking permeates our language, epitomised in phrases such as: "if it ain't broke, don't fix it"; "better the devil you know"; "the grass always appears greener on the other side". These serve as stark warnings for starry-eyed dreamers in search of something better. Even those of us who are more predisposed or open to change will prioritise the things that they really need to be improved – everything else can wait. Therefore, it is probably best to assume that the typical state for most customers is one of inertia; they will stick with what they know. Just as in Newton's First Law of Motion, an object will not change speed or direction unless a force is applied. This principle applies to customers too.

In effect, there are two different forces that start customers on the buying journey: **Compelling Events** or the **Erosion of Satisfaction**.

Compelling Events

A compelling event refers to a change in circumstances, often externally driven, such as: change in regulation or legislation; new market conditions; or competitor activity. Alternatively, internal drivers such as a change in strategy or the implementation of a project can create the event. A compelling event mandates the customer to do something different.

It's worth noting that a compelling event may have already occurred or will occur in the future or may or may not occur at all (but the risks still need to be mitigated).

Erosion of Satisfaction

Erosion of satisfaction generally happens over the longer term and is best described as the difference between desired expectation and experienced reality. Gradually the gap widens to the point where the customer no longer feels that their current situation is sustainable and so they look to change, either with new products, services or suppliers.

It's a phenomenon that customers experience regularly. Most major purchases they make become subject to the erosion of satisfaction over time. This may be due to technological changes that make a product outdated or inferior to later versions, due to deterioration with use or age, or they outgrow past purchases due to gradual changes in their own circumstances.

The widening of the gap between the customer's ideal and current situations doesn't occur overnight and even when it does become noticeable, they typically continue to live with these imperfections until the 'force' of these issues overcomes their inertia.

As such, where erosion of satisfaction is the customer's main driver for change, there can be a lack of urgency. Even where the gap is significant, if they have managed thus far with the current arrangements, waiting to implement something new may not seem like a great hardship, especially in challenging economic times.

STAGE 2 – ESTABLISH NEEDS

Having recognised a compelling event or the erosion of satisfaction, the customer is now 'open to change' or at least, open to exploring possibilities. Their thoughts now turn to understanding and defining what the ideal solution could look like and the criteria by which they can judge the suitability of each potential solution.

Imagine you are looking for a new car. The choice is overwhelming and so you initially narrow down your options to type of car (coupe, saloon, SUV), the size, the characteristics (performance, comfort, efficiency) and any brand references. Even having narrowed it down, you still have a plethora of other factors to consider: equipment, fuel type, hybrid/electric, automatic or manual transmission. From the outset, you will already have started to formulate the criteria against which you can critique each option. This set of criteria is invaluable in enabling you to focus your search and articulate to a potential vendor what your requirements are.

The key activities customers undertake at this second stage include:

- Establishing criteria – we refer to this as the 'wish list'.
- Prioritising criteria – the 'must haves' and 'nice to haves'.
- Researching in more detail and engaging with potential suppliers and vendors.

At this stage the wish list will be restricted by the customer's level of knowledge, assumptions and experience of past decisions. We don't know what we don't know, and therefore the customer's wish list can end up being misaligned with their required outcomes (and budgetary expectations).

STAGE 3 – ASSESS OPTIONS

Having considered the wish list, the customer is now in a position to start reviewing and assessing options; seeing how well different potential solutions match both the list and projected budget.

If they haven't done so already, they may contact potential suppliers for information and seek out proposals, quotations, demonstrations or even product trials. Throughout this stage, the various options will be evaluated against their wish list and either shortlisted or rejected accordingly.

Bear in mind that Stage 2, Establish Needs, and Stage 3, Assess Options, are often iterative processes; as the customer engages with potential vendors, the wish list may evolve. New criteria may be added in the light of their increasing knowledge and awareness, and other factors may be promoted or relegated within the customer's list of priorities.

Although this stage may appear well structured and logical, the reality is that it will be driven by subjective values as much as objectivity. We've seen formal purchasing decisions, driven by procurement, where vendors have been rated against a set of weighted criteria.

This process appears to be clinical until you ask: "Why has price been assigned a forty percent weighting rather than thirty percent or fifty percent?" or: "How did you arrive at an assessment of seven out of ten for that supplier on product quality?"

STAGE 4 – RESOLVE CONCERNS

At some point, having been through Stages 2 and 3, the customer will arrive at a shortlist of options, or potentially just one solution, with which they want to proceed. Whilst these options will represent their preferred solution, they may not be a complete match for the wish list.

At this point the customer should remember that they won't always be able to match every criterion with their final decision. For example, a customer may have a clear idea of the type of home they desire, the preferred location, and the budget they have to work with. Assuming they have been realistic, they can usually manage two out of three (which, as Meatloaf once said, 'ain't bad'!).

In this case, in order to move forward the customer may need to compromise around their ideal solution and re-prioritise key elements of their wish list. Alternatively, they could try and negotiate with the vendor to achieve a better match. Finally, they may have to simply find more budget.

STAGE 5 – COMMIT TO ACTION

This stage may appear relatively simple. It's the point where the customer makes the commitment to move ahead with the solution. Assuming that all the other steps have been dealt with effectively, theoretically this shouldn't pose too many problems; although in reality, it often does.

The psychology of decision making is critically important here and something that we can all relate to. 'Buyer's remorse' is described as the sense of regret following a significant purchase, often manifesting itself even before the product is delivered or experienced. It often comes through doubts which can be exacerbated where the customer has a wealth of options available to them.

Somewhat paradoxically, the more choice and options a customer has before they make a decision, the greater the potential for 'buyer's remorse' following the purchase. However, experience shows that the factors that can impact this post-decision can also impact *pre-decision*.

Fear, uncertainty and doubts (FUDs) that can start to surface include whether:

- The purchase will live up to expectations and deliver the results as promised.
- There is a better or more suitable option available out there.
- The commitment of resources needed for this purchase (which may be more than purely financial) could be better utilised elsewhere.
- The decision may affect the customer's personal standing and reputation.

Imagine the scenario. You're in a restaurant perusing the menu. It all looks great and you hone in on a few options before making your choice. The waiter comes over to take your order, but you're still thinking about the other options, so you ask for a few more minutes. In the end you order your original choice. So, what were those extra few minutes about? It was your 'buyer's remorse' kicking in. It's also the reason why your server will take the menus away once you have ordered, thus reducing the chances of it being changed.

'Buyer's remorse' is not just about the FUD factors, it's also about control, or to be more precise, the lack of it. Over the course of the buying journey, the customer has the perception of being in control. They have identified their needs, created the wish list, reviewed their options and reprioritised. At each stage they've had the choice to continue, stop or go in a different direction. Once they commit, all of those choices cease to be open and the control is lost. Any procrastination is as much about this desire for control than concerns over the solution.

STAGE 6 – ACHIEVE OUTCOMES

The decision to purchase is not the end of the journey. This is because the journey is not about the purchase, as it is for an 'impulse buy', but rather it is about achieving an outcome. Having made a decision, we will be looking at delivery, implementation and results. Some results will become apparent sooner than others and some may never become apparent, for example where the purchase was made to prevent an event from occurring.

Whatever the experience so far, the ultimate judgement will be dictated by the actual achievement of results against the desired or expected return. In the New World, this achievement of results is increasingly important for sellers. The true value of the sale will not be realised without longevity of the contract. The ease with which referrals and references can be shared between potential customers can help or hinder future sales opportunities.

Guiding the Customer through their Journey

Having reviewed the journey, the customer should now consider how the Transformational Seller guides them through their journey. In essence this is what this book is about: providing the skills structures and techniques to enable you, as a seller, to do this effectively.

Here are some of the key elements to consider.

The Start of the Journey

We saw that the first stage was driven by two potential forces: a compelling event or the erosion of satisfaction which dictate both the speed and likelihood of the customer completing their buying journey. When we see sales opportunities getting stuck in the pipeline and losing momentum, decisions being delayed and other customer priorities taking over, it's a sign that the forces driving the customer from the outset weren't significant enough.

Therefore, from the outset the Transformational Seller needs to:

1. Establish any compelling event(s) that the customer has identified and develop a shared understanding of the risks, challenges and opportunities they represent.
2. Understand and explore the gap and probe around any erosion of satisfaction, reviewing how a further widening of this gap over time could impact the achievement of the customer's business goals and outcomes.

It's vital to ensure that the event is *truly* compelling, or that the erosion of satisfaction is significant enough for the customer to commit to the rest of the process, particularly during the later stages when it comes to making the big decision.

Having established the customer's driving reason, the next stage is to fully explore the customer's wish list and uncover the criteria, both the hard factors and the emotive considerations, and understand how the customer and other key stakeholders will be making their decision.

At this stage, the Transformational Seller should use their expertise to advise their customers with respect to the wish list. This involves introducing different criteria that the customer should be considering in addition to reviewing and re-establishing the customer's priorities.

The role of the seller here is to help the customer recognise how well the wish list is aligned to the overall outcomes that they are trying to achieve and how realistic it is within the parameters of their timescale, budget and other resources.

However, perhaps the most important element is enabling the customer to identify the importance of the key elements that differentiate your offering and ensure that they appear high up on their wish list.

Taking it back a Stage – Avoiding the 'Lazy Sale'

It is often only at Stage 3, Assess Options, that the customer engages with potential suppliers. If the customer has already identified their needs, then the temptation here – and we often observe this – is to adopt what we call the 'lazy sale' approach. The assumption is that as the need is already established, both customer and seller can move straight through to Stage 3 and beyond.

The 'Lazy Sale' scenario

The situation usually looks something like this:

- Customer makes contact requesting information about a product or service.
- Seller contacts the customer to confirm requirements.
- Seller delivers a demonstration, creates a proposal or quotation.
- Seller contacts the customer for feedback but gets no response.
- Seller chases numerous times before giving up and closes the opportunity on the customer relationship management (CRM) system. (Reason for loss: no response from client.)
- Seller gets annoyed at the customer for being a 'tyre kicker' and wasting their time.
- Another customer contacts the seller for information and the process repeats itself.

If you've ever found yourself in this scenario or any variation of it (and let's be honest, we all have), then you need to look at the reasons why. It's very easy to see a gift of an opportunity – a customer who expresses a desire to buy – and plough straight ahead to secure a sale as quickly and efficiently as possible. In fact, there's little efficiency in producing a proposal or quotation that goes nowhere, delivering several demonstrations followed by numerous emails or voice messages without response or the repeatedly being told that the customer has yet to make a decision.

The key question is: what was missing from this scenario? Firstly, there was little or no exploration of what created the initial interest for the customer. The seller should have asked what the compelling event or the erosion of satisfaction driving the customer to reach out to potential vendors is. More importantly, is the compelling event or erosion of satisfaction strong enough to see the customer through to the end of their buying journey? If we think that the customer reaching out to us means they are committed to going ahead, then we are likely to be in for a fall.

The problem is compounded by not working through the second stage of the customer buying journey. Failure to explore the thinking behind the customer's wish list, not questioning to test out their assumptions and not using influence and expertise to help prioritise their requirements, leads to pitches and demonstrations that don't capitalise on key differentiators. Because the response is to the same brief as that given to the competition, the proposals and solutions end up being very similar.

When it comes to working through Stage 3, Assess Options, the Transformational Seller:

1. Places emphasis on the outcomes the customer wants to achieve, how their solution solves the problems and issues that have been uncovered during the earlier stages, avoiding the 'feature bashing' approach (i.e., evangelising your solution without linking it to the outcome).
2. Shows how their solution matches the customer's wish list – focusing their pitch around the key decision-making criteria (having explored and influenced their wish list at the previous stage).

As stated, Stages 2 and 3 collectively are an iterative process. The customer, having assessed options, may be better armed with an understanding of what is available and the potential problems they may encounter. Their wish list and prioritisation of criteria is not fixed and can continue to evolve throughout their journey.

One of the unfortunate outcomes from this, however, is that you may be asked to amend your proposal or quotation a number of times to accommodate your customer's evolving thoughts. The better you **Foster Collaboration** and help navigate the customer through Stages 1 and 2, the better position you will be to hit the mark first time, and your proposal will require fewer revisions.

Guiding the Customer Through the Latter Stages

As we move to the latter stages of the buying journey, The Transformational Seller should aim to draw out the customer's concerns. If we know what they are, we can help to resolve them.

Many sellers are reluctant to invite their customers to raise concerns for fear of reinforcing them or that they might talk themselves out of a sale. Whilst that may work for an impulsive transactional sale, in a complex multi-stage process the seller always needs to explore what might hold their customer back from progressing.

It's frustrating when deals stall at this late stage and it's vital to help the customer to move through this phase – the longer it stalls the more likely that the sale will fall away completely.

To achieve this, the Transformational Seller should look to:

1. Encourage the customer to open up about their concerns to understand why they view them in a particular way, and collaborate towards finding a solution.
2. Re-evaluate their wish list – go back to help the customer reconsider and establish what is most important to them, reinforce the reasons why they are

doing this (the compelling need and erosion of satisfaction) and their desired outcomes.

3. Negotiate collaboratively – this doesn't mean automatically dropping the price. The seller should look at how to provide an overall package that still drives the required outcomes, is a better fit for the customer's wish list and still represents a profitable deal for the seller.

4. Review the decision-making process and next steps. Chapter 7 looks at the concept of creating a 'backward plan' with your customer as part of the Discovery Phase and using the key milestones within the plan to maintain momentum at this pivotal stage.

5. Agree on their involvement in relation to these steps (e.g., meeting with key stakeholders).

6. Elevate the risks of not making a positive decision to counter the fear of change. Linked to the backward plan and the customer's overall outcomes, the seller should work through the potential consequences that a delay will have and the increased costs or risks of not acting sooner.

7. Consider how to reduce the perceived loss of control including an emphasis on the ongoing and post-commitment options that the customer will still be involved in. This could include details around add-ons, or further specifications that can be amended. Providing further options enables the customer to feel in control (although the seller should avoid overwhelming the customer with too much choice which can also paralyse decision making).

Beyond the Decision

A fundamental difference between the Transformational Seller and their predecessors is their **sales horizon**. Whilst the Transformational Seller has targets to hit like any other sellers, their mindset for each deal goes beyond the signed contract or purchase order and is aligned to the customer's horizon, the achievement of the outcome.

The Transformational Seller needs to take responsibility during this final stage for:

- Reviewing with the customer how they will measure the success of the purchase.
- Working with them to establish a plan for effective implementation.
- Sharing expertise and know-how from other customer's successes (or failings) to support their customer in effective implementation.

MAJOR CONSIDERATIONS FOR THE CUSTOMER BUYING JOURNEY

The buying journey involves a degree of change for the customer. Change in terms of working with a new partner, in the products and services they utilise, the way in which they purchase these products and services, and potentially the way in which they run their business. Change, as well as being exciting, is often uncomfortable as it runs the risk of opening the FUD gates again!

If we review many of the critical elements that influence the customer buying journey: compelling events, erosion of satisfaction, wish lists; compromises, FUDs; buyer's remorse, it becomes evident that that this journey is driven more by emotion than logic.

Extensive research concludes that emotion trumps logic as a motivator for purchasing decisions, with an ascribed figure as high as eighty-four percent of purchasing decisions being based on emotional factors: 'the head justifies what the heart wants'.

It's often erroneously assumed that this only applies to personal buying decisions and, that in business decisions, logic overrides emotion. It doesn't. When we arrive at work, we don't hand in our emotions at reception and pick them up again on our way out. In our professional lives we get excited, we suffer from stress, we feel energised, we are driven by pride, and crippled by fear and uncertainty.

> No one ever got fired for buying IBM.

Whilst this statement no longer holds the same kind of cache now as it did forty years ago, it's a great reminder of how much emotion (and in this case FUD) can have an impact. It became a self-fulfilling prophecy. IBM, as the technology market leader, became the safe choice for executives having to make major transformational decisions for their business.

Whether it was the best choice or not didn't matter; it was a choice that they were never going to be criticised or sacked for if things went awry. How is this changing in the New World?

Decision making will continue to be driven by emotion. However, these emotional decisions will come under much greater scrutiny from business. Due diligence continues to become stricter. This sees sales cycles potentially lengthen, with more steps and more hoops being added. It will feel easier and more comfortable for customers *not* to make a decision.

Increased competition is likely also to be a feature, particularly during periods of economic uncertainty, with business applying processes and policies that will require more options to be explored and more quotations to be received. Some elements may also go to tender for smaller and less significant projects.

This represents both a risk and an opportunity for sellers, potentially gaining access to sales opportunities that they previously may never have been made aware of. The downside may be the increase in the use of competitor organisations as 'stalking-horses' to support a decision that's already been taken. Unless exercising due care, sellers will spend a lot of time and effort on opportunities that they are never likely to win.

It's important therefore that the Transformational Seller pays close attention to exactly what stage in the buying journey the customer is at, what has got them to this position, who and where the other stakeholders are within the DMU and why they are even in the running.

Now more than ever, strong qualification of precisely where the customer is at on their buying journey, and the factors that are influencing their progress around it, is critical for sellers to understand.

It's also vital that sellers consider how they work with their customer through the buying journey. This is the Transformational Seller's audition – the opportunity to demonstrate the working relationship post-decision and will be key if the purchase is to deliver the customer's desired outcomes.

In that sense, the Transformational Seller increasingly becomes a differentiating factor and a significant part of the value proposition. This sets them apart from their Transactional and Consultative counterparts. The next chapter explores differentiation and value in further detail and, in particular, it looks at how the Transformational Seller becomes the central point of the value proposition.

Exercise: Applying the Customer Buying Journey

Consider a sale that you are currently working through right now, and analyse the customer buying journey in terms of the following:

1. What is the compelling event or erosion of satisfaction that is underpinning the buying journey? How compelling is it? How committed is the customer to making the change?
2. What's on the customer's wish list? How will they be evaluating the different options and what criteria will they be using? How will they prioritise the different criteria and how do the various stakeholders view the priorities differently?
3. What will they be looking for from any proposal or demonstration? What will be the key factors that will make them want to move forward?
4. What FUD factors will get in the way of making this decision? How will you encourage the customer to share them with you? How would you propose to resolve them?

CHAPTER SUMMARY

- The Transformational Seller's role is to collaborate with their customer and guide them around their buying journey, not to try to force them through a sales process. It is therefore vital to understand the key stages of that buying journey and the factors that can influence progress from one stage to the next.
- The customer's **Initial Interest** (Stage 1) is built on either a 'compelling event' or the 'erosion of satisfaction'. Sellers need to explore these at the earliest opportunity to ensure they are strong enough to drive the customer all the way through their buying journey. When opportunities stall, it is almost invariably

because the compelling event or erosion of satisfaction are not strong enough to bring about the change.

- At Stage 2, **Establish Needs**, the customer will begin to construct their 'wish list'. The Transformational Seller should not only seek to understand the key criteria, but also utilise their expertise to help shape and influence these in line with the overall outcomes that the customer is looking to achieve.

- Often customers will only reach out to potential suppliers when they are at Stage 3, **Assess Options**. It's important not to take the 'lazy sale' approach, but instead go back through Stages 1 and 2 with the customer. Ideally sellers should be looking to get involved in Stages 1 and 2 to influence the specification and get ahead of the competition.

- At Stage 4, **Resolve Concerns**, establishing the customer's concerns at the latter stages of the buying journey is essential in moving the opportunity forward. It can feel counter-intuitive to encourage the customer to discuss their reservations, but the Transformational Seller recognises that if they can't see it, and more importantly understand it, then they can't work with the customer to overcome it.

- FUD factors can manifest themselves at any point during the buying journey but often surface at the back end when it comes to Stage 5, **Commit to Action**. To prevent these from inhibiting the sale, the Transformational Seller works with their customer to create a Backward Plan which focuses on the customer's overall outcomes, the engagement required with other stakeholders, and elevates the risk of delay or inaction on the overall goal.

- Step 6 of the buying journey, **Achieve Outcomes**, is concerned with the achievement of outcomes. Whilst this is the horizon for buyers, often sellers don't look past the point where the deal is signed. The Transformational Seller recognises the role that they need to play in enabling the customer to achieve their outcomes, and the business benefits of doing so.

- The customer buying journey is driven largely by emotion. Understanding the emotional drivers for all the stakeholders within the DMU will assist the seller in moving the sale forward.

- In the New World we are seeing greater degrees of scrutiny around purchasing decisions and increased competition as a result of the implementation of more formal decision-making processes. It will therefore be more important than ever to understand and explore the customer's buying journey, to understand whether you, as the seller, are in the running and what you need to do to ensure that you don't become just another supplier.

CHAPTER 4
EXPLODING THE USP MYTH AND THE TRANSFORMATIONAL DIFFERENCE

There are two ways in which an organization can achieve competitive advantage over its rivals: cost advantage and differentiation advantage.

Michael Porter

There are two possible approaches to selling in a competitive market. The first, is to be cheap; the second, is to be different. The Transformational Seller dares to be different.

Unless you can offer products or services which are substantially cheaper than those of your competitors, whilst maintaining a good margin, there is no merit in being the cheapest. Some businesses do achieve a successful cost advantage, but their entire model is built around driving cost out of the business. They benefit from economies of scale that enable the required investment in technology and are often surprisingly innovative in their cost-saving approach.

These businesses increasingly have little need for sales people – automation, AI and enhanced web presence together with effective marketing and branding do the selling for them. They want to remove human contact from the sales process wherever possible, because people are expensive. Sellers who sell based purely on the price advantage of their offering are very much on the endangered species list.

We run an exercise whereby we divide sellers into two groups. We ask one group to see the world through their own company's perspective, and the other to view it through the lens of their customer. We ask each group to identify all the qualities they value and then rank their top three choices in order. Invariably, we get similar results each time, regardless of the sector we are working with. Those who represent their company trot out the same platitudes stated on their website, the same ones that they have been telling their customers for years. These typically include:

good service; dedicated account management; people; technology; innovation; delivery capability; customer services; bandwidth; brand; global reach; one stop shop approach

The groups who put themselves in their customer's shoes often also list some of these qualities. This is because they are unable to detach themselves from their 'supplier centric' thinking. However, the more 'customer centric' groups will come up with relatively abstract traits such as:

reliability; adaptability; flexibility; trustworthiness; demonstrates value

There are two particularly interesting aspects to this exercise:

1. It's rare that either team puts 'price' in their top three, despite many sellers insisting that, 'it's all about price

in our industry'. Therefore, it becomes easy to debunk the myth that customers make purchasing decisions based on price alone.

2. The two groups are rarely aligned. It could be argued that 'good service' links to 'reliability' and 'trustworthiness' but the language and message is wholly inconsistent.

The aim of the exercise is to help sellers appreciate what really matters:

It is not what you believe your Unique Selling Point (USPs) or key differentiators are that is important, but how your customer perceives them.

The value of this difference comes through the specific problems that it solves, balanced against the investment that the customer needs to make. A unique offering is unlikely to gain traction where the cost of the solution outweighs the cost of the problem.

We define value using the value equation:

$$\text{Perceived Difference} \times \text{Problem Solved} = \text{Value}$$

The key word here is 'perceived'. Whatever any seller thinks your company does well or differently is irrelevant if your customer doesn't hold the same view. Perception is reality, and often the customer's perception of difference between one supplier and another is far less distinct than most sellers appreciate. It therefore behoves the Transformational Seller to expand that difference.

Reflecting on our own sales experience, one of the worst things a customer can say is: 'you're all pretty much saying the same thing'. Whilst initially we might feel annoyed with the customer for not recognising the difference, the reality is that if they don't see the difference then it's our fault for not having differentiated significantly enough and built value around these differentiators.

Whilst 'buyer tactics' can also come into play here, if the customer ultimately defaults to price, it's because they don't perceive enough difference to justify paying a premium.

Differentiation and building value: a case study

Bryn: We once worked with a large logistics business and their UK CEO launched our initiative to the whole of his sales team with a statement that still resonates today:

"What I am about to say might shock you. Most of our clients don't give a s**t about our products or services."

He paused and added: "It's the impact on their business that counts."

The delegates were aghast at hearing this, having been encouraged to talk about their 'unique' products and services for years.

For us, it was an enlightened message, and one that many leaders need to take heed of. We then turned the CEO's message into a question, to enable the sales team to apply it: "What makes this company different from other companies in your market?"

There followed the typical 'feature led' conversations around 'e-services', 'track and trace', 'dedicated account management', 'one stop shop' and 'global reach'.

With each supposed USP we asked the group if at least two of their main competitors had similar offerings, to which they answered "yes" each time.

> After several iterations of these 'non-differentiators', they finally
> understood. Over a number of programmes, we worked with this
> company's sales and leadership teams across Europe to change how they
> engaged with their customers. We wanted them to provide a much more
> holistic and client-centric message around the question: How can we
> improve supply chain management?
>
> We simply moved the goalposts to where they had some real
> differentiation.
>
> By questioning what was happening in their customer's business and the
> issues that were preventing the company from achieving its goals, the
> sellers were now able to leverage their expertise and present a tailored and
> impactful solution to achieve desired customer outcomes.
>
> In short, the type of conversations they were now having with their clients
> were different from their those of their competitors.

If you can't demonstrate how you can improve your customer's business, you will always be perceived as a commodity. The customer's decision will either be heavily weighted towards cost, or worse still, it will go to the competitor who is able to convey their value without resorting to price.

Whilst Transactional Sellers can't wait to talk about their solution, the Transformational Seller focuses on a client-centric view of the world. This follows one of Stephen Covey's *7 Habits of Highly Effective People*. They 'seek to understand before being understood'. Knowing where the customer is trying to get to and the potential blockers, is key to successful engagement.

In this case the world of logistics is complex. There are many things that can go wrong, from poor packaging to breakages; theft; late deliveries; and lack of communication with multiple carriers resulting in potential invoicing, tracking, and ownership issues. If things do go wrong, the consequences can be huge. The same can also be said though for any industry!

Differentiation and building value: a case study – continued

Despite the CEO's enlightened approach, other stakeholders needed more convincing.

Before starting the training initiative, their sales director took us to one side and said in no uncertain terms, "no matter what you say, it is all about price in our industry".

This is a self-fulfilling prophecy. If you only ever sell on price, your customers can only buy on price. We decided to test out this assumption by accompanying one of their less-experienced sellers on a day of sales meetings.

The first company we met was a typical prospect: a logistics manager for a manufacturing business. The seller established that they had been working with a local supplier for the past seven years, a decision taken before the manager had joined, and although one of the directors had connections to them, there were no great emotional ties to that supplier.

Whilst the customer was open to discussion, there didn't seem to be any compelling reason for them to want to change (besides being tempted with a huge discount).

So, we asked a question: "What changes or improvements would better help you to achieve your outcomes?"

The client stopped and thought for a moment before responding with great frustration. "Well, the supplier never communicates with us!"

He expanded further, describing how vehicles often arrived unscheduled and unannounced. This meant that he would need to take people off the production line to help with unloading, thus halting the production line. Sometimes trucks would be turned away and re-scheduled. It was becoming a real challenge. He'd had several conversations with the supplier, but nothing had changed. We then asked about the consequences for him personally. He gave his answer thus: "aside from the heat I get from the business, I'm sometimes here until seven-thirty or eight-thirty at night and I don't get paid overtime. I have two young children at home, and they are often in bed when I get in, which means I miss out on spending time with them or reading them a bedtime story."

Here was a customer who recognised the business and personal imperative of making the change, the ultimate impact was that he was missing out on vital family time.

After just one short meeting it wasn't difficult to go back to the sales director and tell him, at the very first attempt, we had found a customer for whom it wasn't 'all about price'.

Difference is about perception. Just as customers may not perceive the actual differences between your offering and the competition's, the reverse may also be true.

It is well known that supermarkets will offer own-label brands that are in fact manufactured by the brand leaders in the same factories, to the same recipes and production processes. This is no secret. Yet shoppers will still pay a premium for the branded product, swearing blind that they can taste the difference.

Therefore, your options to differentiate are not just bound by your offering, but how you choose to develop, package and support it.

The Transformational Seller adds value to the customer's business by making it more successful. In essence, differentiation is not always about having the capability to do something that the competition can't do; it comes through asking the right questions and uncovering the customer's real needs.

THE FOUR-LEVEL MODEL FOR DIFFERENTIATION

As we have seen, without strong differentiation, our offering becomes more commoditised, negotiation is extremely challenging, and margins get eroded.

However, with the advancement in technology and information, few organisations have what could be described as USPs.

If they do, they don't generally have them for very long. Shorter development times and rapid speed to market now mean that new product development and enhancements in service offerings are quickly replicated or superseded by the competition.

Differentiation is an ever-moving target for the seller who wants to avoid getting caught in the 'commodity trap' and delivering just another 'me too' offering. Business is now as much an art as a science and, when considering how to stand out from the herd, it's increasingly about the abstract rather than the exact; less about features and more about capability.

Therefore, differentiation can be considered to exist on four levels – ranging from the defined to the undefined, from top to bottom.

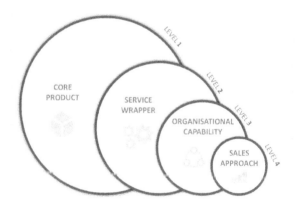

Figure 4.1: The Four-Level Model for Differentiation

LEVEL 1 – CORE PRODUCT OR SERVICE

Here the focus is based on the more traditional features of your product or service. It's still about expressing the differences (albeit subtle differences) that define your offering ahead of the competition.

For example, your product has a 'widget' attached that provides functionality which other products don't. Perhaps it is faster, more accurate, or lasts longer, and by linking these aspects to the customer's required outcomes and potential pains, this feature provides you with a competitive advantage.

These product advantages rarely last. The moment you start to gain real market share, the competition inevitably responds with their new and improved product. It's vital that sellers monitor competitor activity and that organisations continue to develop and innovate to give their teams the tools needed to build value.

LEVEL 2 – SERVICE WRAPPER

It's not just the product that provides the opportunity to differentiate, but also the 'service wrapper' that accompanies it. Service wrappers are the add-ons that may not be part of the actual package, but which enable the client to take delivery of the product or service and, more importantly, optimise their purchase. This might include installation, user training, technical support or project management. These activities enable the customer to gain quicker or easier access to the outcomes that your product or service provides.

This is where many businesses are able to innovate and develop their overall proposition, although as with the product, the situation can change quickly. We worked with one business who, having invested in new technology and infrastructure, could guarantee next day delivery for products ordered before 3pm.

This was a real coup for their sales team: the ability to respond faster to meet their customers changing needs. Within months, their largest competitor was offering the same service for orders placed before 5pm. Pretty soon, 'same day ordering' had entered the market and rendered their USP obsolete.

Six Minute Abs!

This issue is perfectly illustrated by a scene in the film *There's Something about Mary* when a bemused Ben Stiller is asked to invest in a deranged backpacker's 'sure fire investment opportunity'.

"You've heard of the video 'Eight Minute Abs? Well, I'm going to produce a 'Seven Minute Abs' video," the backpacker claims.

He then proceeds to fly into a rage when Stiller's character questions what will happen if someone then produces a 'Six Minute Abs' video!

LEVEL 3 – ORGANISATIONAL CAPABILITY

Here, differentiation enters into a more abstract realm and is less about the tangible and clearly defined specifics of the product or accompanying service wrapper.

By considering organisational capability, we explore the broader, more holistic offering that your business can provide. This might include aspects such as R&D investment, national or global presence, a local branch network, or a more extensive range of product and service offerings.

The challenge here is that these form part of the traditional 'credentials' presentation. You may be familiar with 'impressive' slides that show your prospect what a great organisation they are about to partner with. The trouble with most of these is that they don't pass the 'so what' test, as they are often largely irrelevant to the immediate needs of your customer.

The key to enabling these to give you a genuine competitive edge, is to broaden the conversation with your customer onto a more strategic level. By opening up the discussion to include your customer's longer-term goals, aims and objectives, you will be able to highlight the relevance of your organisational capability to their purchasing decision.

Their needs will change over time and by demonstrating that the purchase they are making today is future proofed against these changing needs, you can demonstrate that the knowledge of their changing needs can be integrated into the purchases that they will make going forward. This enables previously abstract and irrelevant boasts to now become critical to their thinking.

In the New World, purchasing decisions will be about long-term partnership as much as short-term need and those areas that demonstrate your ability to be the long-term partner for your customer.

LEVEL 4 – SALES APPROACH

The deepest level of differentiation is all about you, the Trans-formational Seller. Whilst it's true that it is better to start a business relationship by being liked rather than loathed, many sellers over-emphasise the importance of getting on well with the customer on a personal level. A note of caution, this doesn't mean that you shouldn't be trying to build rapport; it's simply that creating a sound business relationship requires much more.

The key to enabling yourself to be the differentiator is to be 'The Expert', which means:

- Reviewing what your customers really need, not simply what they think they need.
- Encouraging the customer to think differently.
- Identifying problems that they weren't aware of.

- Coaching the customer towards a better, more rounded solution.

The Transformational Seller thrives in this area as they are able to utilise their expertise throughout the sales process to wow the customer and create those 'moments' during the sales process that offer so much value to the customer.

Your Expertise – Becoming the Catalyst for Change

The price of expertise (a parable)

For years, a steamboat owner operating his vessel on the Mississippi ran his boat up and down the river, carrying hundreds of passengers a day and making a lot of money in the process. One day, he went to start up the engine and nothing happened.

Perplexed, he sent for an engineer to come and fix the boat, but they couldn't find the problem. He sent for several other engineers but none were able to get the engine working. By now the steamboat owner was losing thousands of dollars a day and was prepared to offer huge sums to anyone who could fix his boat.

After a week an elderly engineer arrived at the boat yard.

"I've come to fix your boat," he said. "But I'm warning you, I don't come cheap!"

"That's ok," said the owner. "If you can get this boat running it will be worth it."

So, the engineer made his way into the engine room and examined the various pipes and valves, tapping with his hand and pressing his ear up against them.

Eventually he settled next to a large pipe, opened up his tool bag, took out a large wooden mallet and gave the pipe a firm tap. Instantly the engine sprang into life to the delight of the owner. The broad smile that appeared on his face soon turned sour when the engineer handed him the invoice.

"$10,000 for that!" the owner exclaimed. "How can you justify $10,000 for just one tap of your mallet?"

"Would it help if I provided you with a breakdown of the cost?" asked the engineer. He took back the invoice, scribbled some notes on it and thrust it back into the owner's hand.

The owner looked down, smiled and nodded:

- Cost of tapping engine with the mallet: $1.
- Cost of knowing where to tap: $9,999.

Professional advisers, such as accountants or lawyers, are given their status because they have established expertise in their specific field and can provide information and guidance on what to do and, just as importantly, what to avoid.

We rely on them, not because we're stupid (although sometimes we are), but because we can't know everything about everything. In fact, we can't even know a lot about a lot, but we can know a lot about something. That is where the Transformational Seller shines, because they do know a lot about something.

That *something* is more than product knowledge. In fact, transactional sellers often have excellent product knowledge and that is often part of the problem, as they focus their entire sales effort on transferring their product knowledge onto their prospect.

The Transformational Seller has built their knowledge and expertise from:

- Their understanding of their products and services.
- Their experience of the industry and the changes that are taking place.
- Their knowledge of the typical problems and issues that customers face.
- Their experience of the successes and failures that other customers have had.

The great news is that whilst expertise takes years to develop, even relatively new or inexperienced sellers have the capacity to develop and deliver expertise.

Every time you engage with a customer and see how they have overcome various problems and issues; you are building up your reservoir of knowledge and expertise which can be used for the benefit of future customers.

Combine this with case studies your organisation has developed within your existing customer base and you will quickly be able to bring value to your conversations. Link these back to the outcomes your current customer is looking to achieve and you are well on the way to becoming a Transformational Seller.

Naked in Helsinki – monetising the solution

Bryn: I was once in Helsinki working with a tech company specialising in energy management systems for the shipping industry. Along with their team, who had come from all over the world, we took over the top floor of the Radisson Hotel. This was part of their annual conference.

It's a trip I'll never forget, as it's the only time I have ever been stark naked with my delegates on Day One (or Two for that matter!). When I was introduced to the CEO, we were both wearing only a smile as we shook hands. Before you get too concerned, this was at the end of the working day in Finland, and this is perfectly normal behaviour for the Finnish (note, the men and women had separate sauna sessions).

Shortly before this and whilst still fully clothed, a couple of the directors asked me if I could critique their sales teams' presentations, to which I readily agreed. As their four key account managers gave me their highly technical presentations, two things struck me. Firstly, had I been asked during the day to state which of the delegates were in non-commercial as opposed to commercial roles, I would have been unable to tell them apart. Secondly, whilst their technical and industry knowledge were all consistently brilliant, there was nothing really compelling in any of their presentations, least of all the two percent saving a client could make if they installed their software (which helped steer ships in the most economical direction as well as providing vital management information back to shore).

I queried the two percent, as it didn't sound like much. I asked: "What's the cost of fuel typically for a ship?"

"Around 180 tonnes a day at $120 per tonne," came the reply.

"How many days a year does a cruise or cargo ship sail?" was my next question.

"Around six months of the year on average."

"And how many ships will a typical operator own?"

"It varies considerably, but fifteen to twenty-five would be a reasonable number."

I did a quick calculation and worked out that they could be saving companies up to $4m a year on an investment of around $350k per installation. When I relayed this back, they looked at me like I was Einstein solving the Theory of Relativity before their own eyes.

Monetising a solution based on annual or even lifetime usage can have an extremely powerful effect. Four million sounds a lot more impressive than two percent even if both figures are factually correct. Few companies do this well, and it's hard to comprehend why – and when it is done there's a tendency for sellers to approximate the figures. Ideally, you should get the customer to do the maths. A key part of fostering collaboration is to ask the questions and let the customer fill in the blanks. It's more powerful when it's their numbers that go into the mix.

Exercise: Establishing your Differentiators

Consider the 'value equation', Perceived Difference x Problem Solved = Value, and carry out the following:

- List what you see as your perceived differentiators.
- Speak to a sample of your customers you have engaged with recently and ask them why they chose to buy from you (ideally choose those clients where you were in a competitive situation).
- Review how aligned your list of differentiators are with the customer's reasons for choosing to work with you.

You should look to make this exercise an important part of the regular communication with your customers. Whenever you win a deal, take time out to get feedback from your customer as to why you won it. This is probably more valuable information than trying to understand why you lost deals, and you are far more likely to get an honest answer!

CHAPTER SUMMARY

- The only two ways to gain competitive advantage are to be cheaper or different. Selling on price results in a devalued brand, increased commoditisation, much tougher negotiations and lower margins. Businesses will have little need for transactional price-led sellers in the New World.
- The Transformational Seller creates value by demonstrating the difference they can bring and the problem they can solve for their customer (in achieving their overall outcomes). The greater this outweighs the price, the more value this demonstrates.
- Sellers and suppliers tend to trot out similar platitudes whilst claiming them to be USPs. Ironically, they are often neither unique and – unless they relate to a specific outcome the customer is looking to achieve or a

problem that is holding them back –they aren't a selling point either.

- Differentiation comes at four different levels: the product, the service wrapper, organisational capability, and finally, your expertise (the way that you sell). The last is the most important of all the four and is a key Transformational Seller trait.
- Monetisation of a solution or a problem in relation to the achievement or non-achievement of an outcome is pivotal in demonstrating value and building the business case for change.

CHAPTER 5
THE TRANSFORMATIONAL MINDSET

Can't start a fire without a spark.

Bruce Springsteen

Figure 5.1: The Transformational Triumvirate

Just as there are three elements needed to start a fire, there are three key attributes required to sustain the Transformational Seller Approach: **knowledge**, **skills** and **mindset**. In each subsequent chapter we show you how to leverage your knowledge as expertise and develop your Transformational skills. It's important that we first acknowledge the importance of **mindset** within the Transformational Triumvirate.

Many organisations focus their sales training around knowing the product inside out. Therefore, it's not surprising that most sellers score well on knowledge. Sales skills, on the other hand, tend to be neglected. Yet, despite the paucity of effective skills development and coaching within these organisations, we see successful performers. These sellers are not always those with the best skills. Rather, they possess what we call the 'spark'. Without this spark, skills and knowledge remain untapped. In other words, their mindset.

As you go through the chapters in this book you are likely to come across concepts and ideas that may seem difficult or uncomfortable to implement. That's a good thing!

If an idea is difficult and feels uncomfortable, the majority of sellers will shy away from implementing it. They will continue with their existing approach. They will carry on asking the same questions, present their well-rehearsed pitches, deliver their highly choreographed demonstrations and, when all else fails, discount heavily to try and win the deal.

Our message is simple: if it feels uncomfortable, then do it.

'COMFORT ZONE' VERSUS 'ACTION ZONE' SELLING

We live in a paradoxical world where differing political and religious ideologies cause conflict and yet, despite this, most people prefer to avoid conflict wherever possible.

The concept of the Comfort Zone is linked to social norms regarding what is acceptable behaviour. It relates to our tendency to tell 'white lies' to avoid upsetting people, to not ask intrusive questions and to exercise caution in expressing views that may challenge others. Whilst these behaviours might assist us in keeping social interactions away from conflict, they don't help us from a sales perspective.

If Transformational Selling is about assisting your customer to achieve their goals through eliminating the barriers and inefficiencies within their current situation, it's going to require some degree of discomfort. The golden rule of sales is that if your customer is sitting comfortably, they have no reason to change.

The counter to the idea of the 'Comfort Zone' is the 'Action Zone', where life is less comfortable for you and the customer. Without discomfort we don't see action and we don't experience change. Some of the key differences between the two are broken down in Table 5.1.

	Comfort Zone Selling	Action Zone Selling
Networking	Over-reliance on selling to an existing customer base or engaging only with established contacts. Failure to network with more senior decision makers.	Actively seeking more contacts and connections, engaging with more stakeholders (particularly those at a more senior level).

	Comfort Zone Selling	Action Zone Selling
Servicing	Whilst 'going the extra mile' is viewed positively, many sellers offer regular free assistance and support for their customers under the misapprehension that this increases loyalty leads to more sales. There can be a tendency to give things away as part of the sales process – free samples, extra time, product trials and proof of concepts – without establishing clear success criteria.	Ensuring that there is some form of 'quid pro quo' for the work carried out. If you are going to offer the customer a free trial or sample, you need to have agreed specific criteria around what constitutes success and have established a plan following a successful proof of concept in return.
Relationships	Although having good customer rapport is highly desirable, it's not the same as having an excellent business relationship. Knowing your client's favourite sports team or their children's names as the sole approach for relationship development is not going to be an effective business strategy.	The most critical element is understanding the customer's business drivers, their success measures and desired business and personal outcomes – including how they are measured and rewarded.

	Comfort Zone Selling	Action Zone Selling
Commitment	Agreeing to send literature, put together a quotation, or offer to write time-consuming proposals, without any real commitment from the customer to play their part. Eager to please and happy to do something for the client without asking for anything in return. Here, the commitment is passive.	Testing the customer's level of desire and commitment by expecting something in return: whether that be their time, introducing other stakeholders, access to sensitive information or an agreement towards a plan.
Order-taking	Waiting to be asked for something by the customer and then only providing what they've requested to keep the customer on-side during the sales process. Not wanting to rock the boat or risk damaging the relationship by exploring other possibilities.	Broadening the conversation, up-selling, cross-selling or identifying a more holistic solution. Questioning to explore why the customer has made the request and ensuring they have understood what they are looking to achieve in the long term.

	Comfort Zone Selling	Action Zone Selling
Account management	Acting as 'account maintenance executives', performing functions which should be delegated to customer services or technical support, failing to get higher and wider within an account and ignoring potential 'C Level' contacts.	Being focused on how to grow an account and take income and profitability to the next level. Supporting the achievement of customer outcomes, driving more strategic conversations and establishing their longer-term business objectives.
Prospecting	The advent of 'Social Selling' has changed the communication landscape and 'social networking' has become hugely significant. However, over reliance on sending emails or messaging as the mainstay of prospecting is a sign of a seller wanting to avoid the discomfort that comes with more two-way customer interactions.	The use of Social Selling, email and other forms of interaction are components of good prospecting, but only as part of a holistic strategy that includes making calls, virtual meetings and face-to-face communication. It's almost impossible to change viewpoints, handle difficult situations, negotiate effectively, or gain active commitments, without speaking to a customer.

Comfort Zone Selling	Action Zone Selling
Not rocking the boat	Wanting to be liked and shying away from asking tough questions, avoiding making suggestions and readily agreeing to customer demands. A hesitance to make phone calls for fear of appearing intrusive, having awkward conversations, or ending up in conflict situations.	Being cognisant that comfortable fireside chats rarely deliver sound business benefits. Understanding that unless the customer sees value, they will view such contacts as a luxury their busy schedules won't allow. Instead, deriving value from more challenging interactions and gaining new and different perspectives, by suggesting different ways of working referrals into other divisions or stakeholders.

Table 5.1 Comfrot Zone versus Action Zone Selling

The Comfort Zone seller isn't lazy. They often work long hours, travel huge distances, write countless proposals and prepare endless quotations. They appear to work hard but, in reality, they just work long: working this way is so much easier than questioning to establish how serious the client is about working with them or asking them for something in return.

As introduced in Chapter 2, we have termed this **The Labrador Effect**. No matter how far the customer metaphorically throws the slipper, the seller always runs to retrieve it. This often includes devaluing their service by offering non-standard items or normally chargeable work for free.

We are not advocating that sellers should provide a less-than-great service; it's simply that they shouldn't rely on this approach to achieve quota (whilst deluding themselves that they are constantly busy and productive).

In the New World there will be little room for sentiment and loyalty in customer decision making. Any tactic that relies solely on the customer reciprocating good will is likely to fail.

Facing conflict: flight or fight response

Bryn: As a young sales executive my first boss often used me as a 'guinea-pig' to launch new products. At the time I was selling artificial surfaces and sports pitch projects. One day he handed me a small piece of white carpet.

"It's a new type of ski-surface that will revolutionise the artificial ski-slope market. I want you to find a site that will agree to trial it," my boss explained to me.

The market at the time was dominated by a product called Dendix, a diamond-shaped bristle with gaps in the middle. When skiers fell on this surface, they risked trapping their hands in the gaps and injuring themselves.

The following day I headed up to the nearby ski centre, walked into the manager's office and placed the sample on his desk.

"This is a new artificial ski surface that will greatly reduce injuries," I announced confidently.

I can't print his reply, but the second word was 'off'! When I didn't move, he repeated the invective, only this time more aggressively. I was rooted to the spot, shocked by his outburst.

"I apologise if I've offended you, but can you please explain what I've done wrong?" I asked.

"In addition to being the centre manager here I'm also the secretary of the British Ski Association, and every new surface that enters this country has to be vetted by me. I've never seen this before, so you've clearly not gone through the proper channels."

There were two ways to view this: either walk away with my tail between my legs and accept that I should have done more research on my prospect or appreciate that this was an amazing stroke of luck – landing on the very person who could approve and endorse this product.

It was 'fight or flight' time. Not wanting the humiliation of telling my boss that I had fallen at the first hurdle, I chose to fight. This was my response: "I appreciate that and apologise, but before I go, I'd be really interested in your views, particularly in relation to the safety of children when using your facilities."

Two hours and a few phone calls later, the manager agreed to trial the new product (at cost price) on his nursery slope. I still remember that meeting now, thirty-five years later. It marked a seminal moment in my career.

PUTTING IT INTO PERSPECTIVE

Many of the skills and approaches that we teach through our programmes require delegates to make the leap from the Comfort Zone to the Action Zone: we carry out an exercise which put delegates' fears around selling into perspective.

We start by getting them to think about major negative events that could happen in their lifetime. We ask them to give the events a rating on a scale of 1–10 (where 10 = death). We then ask them to assign a number from this scale based on some more personal events:

- Being declared bankrupt.
- A relationship breakup.

- Losing a limb.

Bankruptcy averages around a 5 or 6. A relationship break-up can be anything from a 1 to a 7 depending upon circumstances. The answer to the third question averages around an 8, although the lowest we have ever heard is a 2.

When asked why, the delegate in question told us about a friend of his who had returned from Rio in 2016 having won a silver medal in the Paralympics. This friend had previously lost his leg in Afghanistan. After winning the silver, the friend had said that he probably wouldn't have his leg back even if he could. Without that tragedy he wouldn't have become a Paralympic medal winner.

That is a mindset shift of epic proportions!

Next, we ask the delegates to consider that given these three major events relate to health, wealth and love – aspects of life most people would consider vitally important – where they would next place making a call to a new prospect or having a challenging conversation with an existing customer. Set against the context of these other more fundamental issues this never scores higher than a 1 or 2, and we sometimes also get minus numbers. This exercise serves to reduce the fear factor in the way that delegates approach sales.

Many people hate the idea of having to call someone they have never spoken to before, or the thought of having a difficult conversation with a client about an issue or complaint they have raised. However, once they have conducted the call, when asked how it went the answer is almost invariably: "oh, much better than I thought it would."

The power of belief

Steve: We once worked with a company who were market leaders within their industry. However, whilst they rarely lost customers, their record in attracting new business was mixed. Being in a niche area, traditional marketing methods were unlikely to drive many enquiries. They needed their sales team to proactively prospect.

On meeting the sales team, the sellers highlighted the usual challenges with prospecting, including the following: people didn't want to speak to them, they were too busy to meet, the gatekeepers were being instructed not to put them through and the customers were happy with their current suppliers.

These were smokescreens; excuses for why the sellers shouldn't be prospecting. When we explored this further, the group started to open up. Their problem was borne out of the belief that cold calling was an intrusion into a customer's working day and that they were a nuisance. There was therefore a reticence to make such calls.

Whilst we could teach them the skills needed to make an effective call it would be futile without first dealing with their limiting belief.

Changing beliefs isn't easy. Rather than persuade them that their call was not an intrusion, we instead focused on finding an empowering belief to anchor their approach. Therefore, we focused them on the one thing that they had unwavering confidence in: their offering.

We put the issue of cold calling to one side and got the sellers to work in groups. We asked them to answer the following questions:

- Why do your best/most loyal customers continue to buy from you?
- What are the key business benefits they gain from working with you?
- How does this compare with the benefits of your competitors?

Having considered these, we posed one final question: "Based on your answers, why are your prospects not currently buying from you?"

Their main conclusion was that prospects didn't know about their offering and the difference that they could provide. The empowering belief came when one of the team announced: "We have something potentially very valuable to offer prospects. We have the right to make that call!"

"I think it's more than just the right to make the call," added another. "I think we have a duty to make the call!"

Now that's an empowering belief.

After working on their call structure, we challenged them to call potential prospects. Typically, they would make around a dozen new business appointments a month collectively; over the afternoon session the team booked fifty-five new business meetings.

THE MINDSET OF A TRANSFORMATIONAL SELLER

With market turbulence and uncertainty, Transformational Sellers recognise the need to change their prospecting approach, whether they cast their net wider or focus on a particular market sector that is still spending. In short, they respond to the conditions.

When up against cheaper competition, these sellers focus their efforts on building value, emphasising the importance of their differentiators and questioning the implications of relying on a less effective solution.

"We lost it on price boss."

These are the words every sales director hears from their team time and again. Sellers with limiting beliefs tend to have fixed opinions such as 'price is everything'.

The Transformational Seller explores the potential ramifications of customers making price-driven decisions. The impact of clients not delivering for their own customers could be astronomical and the damage irreparable. By focusing on such risks, they act as the catalyst to spark a radical rethink. If the customer goes for a cheaper option, the Transformational Seller accepts that they didn't build enough value and weren't able to bridge the gap. They learn from this and move on.

Transformational Sellers are comfortable asking difficult questions, even if this may be uncomfortable for the customer. To restate: if you are sitting comfortably, you have no reason to change. The Transformational Seller is driven by the desire to make their customer's business better, and in the process their customer's customer, to ensure all parties achieve their outcomes. Once able to evidence this, the customer is likely to remain loyal and open to expanding the relationship further.

There are so many factors that influence the selling environment: competition, economy, brand recognition, price point, procurement policies, existing supplier relationships, contracts, reputation, customer awareness. All of these can assist or hinder our sales efforts.

If selling was easy, if customers fully recognised their needs, if sellers were always able to offer the perfect solution at the cheapest price, if the economy was strong, if money was no object and if there was no competition, then businesses wouldn't need to employ sales people and they certainly wouldn't need to reward them with high earnings.

A winning mind set – when attitude trumps experience

Bryn: I worked for many years in sales recruitment in the IT sector. During that time, I interviewed over 3,000 people. A 'star performer' is someone who has a real belief in their ability, backed by strong supporting evidence. I would rate no more than five percent of the people I interviewed in this category.

I once ran a campaign for a national sales manager for a government defence role. Most of the applicants had a strong background in defence. In those days, I often met with clients and prospects in clubs around London. The term for this is the 'old boys' network'.

One applicant had far less experience than the others but through sheer persistence, made it to the final interview stage. I asked him what he thought he could bring to the role. His response was: "I used to be a professional squash player in Pakistan, and I became a Top 10 world ranked player: I'd now like to do the same within the IT sector." Not only did he blow away all the other far more 'relevant' candidates, he was also an enormous success, being highly driven and extremely charismatic. A case of attitude and will trumping experience.

Exercise 1: Comfort Zone versus Action Zone

For each of the eight criteria highlighted in the table in this chapter, rate yourself on a scale of 1–5 as to whether you feel the Comfort Zone or Action Zone descriptions best describes your approach. A score of 1 represents 'predominantly acts in Comfort Zone' and a 5 represents 'predominantly acts in the Action Zone'.

For which areas are you straying too far into the Comfort Zone?

What can you do differently to be more 'Action Zone' orientated?

Exercise 2: Gaining Perspective

Using the perspective exercise in this chapter, rate the following 1–10 in terms of seriousness or impact:

- A major health issue.
- A serious financial problem.
- A relationship break up.

Next, assign a number to an 'uncomfortable' activity that you know you should be doing more of (e.g., prospecting, cross-selling, getting to more senior stakeholders etc) and compare against the other three criteria.

Then act on it!

CHAPTER SUMMARY

- The core attributes of a Transformational Seller are a mix of **knowledge**, **skills** and **mindset**. Their mindset is a combination of attitude, beliefs and response to their environment.
- 'Comfort Zone' sellers demonstrate a lack of networking, and over-servicing instead of actually selling. **The Labrador Effect** creates a master–servant relationship as opposed to a genuinely collaborative business–partner one.
- Transformational Sellers are responsible for adapting and developing their approach in response to the external events around them. They make the necessary changes required to deliver results. If the customer opts for a cheaper solution, they recognise that they didn't build enough value and learn from that.
- The perspective exercise can be useful as it enables sellers to reduce the fear factor and move from a **Comfort Zone** to an **Action Zone**. It places a fresh perspective on what might otherwise seem uncomfortable to them.

CHAPTER 6
OPENING UP THE OPPORTUNITY

People who can focus, get things done.

People who can prioritise, get the right things done.

John Maeda

FINDING THE RIGHT DIRECTION

When we created the Managed Services Division at Pareto well over a decade ago, focusing on bespoke sales training and assessment, our first instinct was to target the big IT players, such as Microsoft, Cisco and HP. After all, these were major organisations with large sales teams and reputations for investing in their development.

Our prospecting team did a good job at opening doors with these companies. However, we soon realised three critical factors:

- Unsurprisingly, many competitors were also targeting these companies.
- They already had global development programs in place and resources to deliver internally.
- Because of the nature of the geographies and number of stakeholders involved, the sales process was complex.

Whilst this didn't stop us (we eventually worked with all three), we saw greater success in what we perhaps unflatteringly termed the 'oily rags market'. This is not meant to be disparaging. We worked with some great businesses in manufacturing, logistics and construction. They all had the following in common:

- Their product or services was viewed as a commodity by clients where differentiation was hard to demonstrate.
- Their margins were perilously low, and price was a frequent objection.
- Their sales teams contained many 'Comfort Zoners' with little formal training.
- Their managers were generally ex-sellers with no real coaching experience.
- Their sales teams demonstrated significant limiting beliefs with respect to prospecting, cross selling and negotiating.

These issues were in our sweet spot. Many of the companies we dealt with had large sales teams, the vast majority of whom were underperforming at the time (in 2009, just after the financial crisis).

Once we got in front of them, it wasn't difficult to identify some of the challenges they were facing, create a compelling event or accelerate the erosion of satisfaction. We then focused on developing their wish list, the 'why choose us' argument, and then progressed the opportunity.

It is critical at the outset to understand and define your target market and your ideal customer profile (ICP). It's easy to operate a 'scattergun' approach to lead generation as opposed to being more strategic as to where you focus. You should use historical data, business case studies and innovative thinking to find answers to the following:

- Which companies have you had the most success with? (i.e., where you have helped to achieve their desired outcomes).
- What problems have you solved?
- Who else could be experiencing similar problems?

COLLABORATING INTERNALLY

Some might say that lead generation is purely a function of marketing.

Traditionally, marketing departments have been responsible for broader communication and large distribution, with sales departments focusing on communicating directly with individuals (i.e., marketing departments send out a mass email and sales departments conduct the follow-up calls).

This distinction, however, is becoming increasingly blurred. Automation and AI are already enabling marketing departments to tailor and personalise messaging to individual prospects. Simultaneously, social media such as LinkedIn and Twitter have enabled individual sellers to access a wider audience and develop both their own and their organisations' brand.

As the boundaries merge, so the collaboration between the two needs to increase.

BUSINESS OPPORTUNITY CREATION – A FOUR STAGE APPROACH

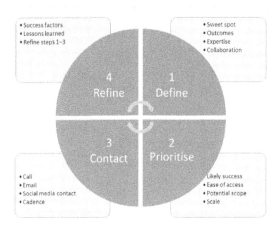

Figure 6.1: Business Opportunity Creation – A Four Stage Approach

STAGE 1 – DEFINE

This first stage is about defining the 'sweet spot', in other words, what makes a good prospect. The traditional answer is often based around whoever has the deepest pockets or the largest scalability for your offering, but the reality has to trade effort versus reward.

Prospecting with a Transformational mindset means considering:

- **Outcomes** – which businesses would you be able to deliver the best outcomes for? This may be based on the overall outcomes the customer typically wants to achieve, the problems they could be facing and your

experience and history of overcoming similar problems
for customers.

- **Expertise** – based on the outcomes. Where do you have
  the ability to bring expertise to customers? Again,
  looking at certain sectors may be useful but also
  thinking around which organisations are likely to be
  missing that expertise internally and asking why.
- **Collaboration** – which organisations are most likely to
  work collaboratively with you as a partner as opposed
  to working as just a supplier? Who is likely to be a good
  fit based on their company ethos, their strategies and
  culture?

STAGE 2 - PRIORITISE

The second stage focuses on looking at which of the leads identified represent the best fit against the sweet spot. The factors
you will need to consider are:

- **Likely success** – which organisations can you have the
  greatest impact with? Note that success in this area is
  defined as: 'who we can deliver the best outcomes for'
  as opposed to 'who it will be easiest to get a meeting
  with'.
- **Ease of access** – where can you have conversations with
  the right people? Referrals and recommendations play
  their part in this step. If you can be introduced or
  referred into a business, then you significantly increase
  the chance of speaking to the people you need to be
  influencing.
- **Potential scope** – businesses have greater scope if they
  require the use of your full range of services. Those
  whose outcomes potentially need a wider cross-section

of your products are more likely to become longer-term collaborative business partners.

- **Scale** – what's the potential size of the ultimate prize? Usually, larger businesses will have greater scalability for your offering, but this needs to be balanced against the likelihood of success, ease of access and speed of decision making.

(Note, it amazes us how few companies seek regular recommendations or referrals from their clients and contacts – those are almost always 'A Grade leads'.)

STAGE 3 – CONTACT

Already we see prospecting becoming more sophisticated and recognised as such. Moving away from trawling through lists and following calling scripts, some prospectors are becoming mini-marketers, developing content and using a multi-channel approach to open up conversations.

Picking up the phone and engaging directly is still critical, but as part of a more co-ordinated approach to attract attention.

In opening up opportunities, it's important to identify a number of stakeholders within your target company as opposed to a single individual. The more stakeholders you can engage with, or at least be aware of, the greater the chance of success. Important decisions are increasingly made by 'committee' not individuals; the earlier you engage with multiple stakeholders the better you can **foster collaboration** and influence how they interact collectively as a DMU.

This helps to reduce those potential 'spanners in the works' that everyone experiences when a (usually) more senior stakeholder puts a halt on the process, wants different outcomes, or has a preference for another supplier to your key sponsor.

'Early-stage collaboration' helps to define the various objectives and outcomes for each stakeholder and assists you in navigating the potential conflicts which can occur at a later stage. Whilst it may not always be possible to get a whole DMU in a room together, you can nevertheless leverage your sponsors' understanding of the situation and, wherever possible, meet with more than one person.

Typical activities within the initial contact stage will include interaction on social media, direct communications via email, sending videos and, ultimately, making a phone call.

The reality is that you will need to combine all of these with some form of discipline or structure – you rarely get a response to your first email or voicemail. You may not get put through when you ring the first, second, or even third time.

This multi-stage approach requires the discipline of a 'cadence' which looks at developing a sequence of engagements over a period of time, using a combination of communication channels to start a dialogue with the prospect.

The death of cold calling?

Mark Twain reportedly sent a telegram back home after reading his own obituary in a newspaper that read: "the reports of my death are greatly exaggerated."

Many people tell us that cold calling is dead and it simply isn't true. What is dying out and will become extinct in the New World, is the old-school tele-marketer bashing through call lists with a script and a smile without giving the prospect any good solid reason to engage.

Picking up the phone in the B2B world will continue, as part of an integrated communications strategy, but it will have a much more targeted and clearly defined purpose.

Engaging with Prospects

This book is not intended to focus on prospecting, cold calling, social media selling or getting through gatekeepers, which is a vast and complex subject in its own right. There are many specialist books with much more specific advice, hints and tips available. Our recommendations include *Fanatical Prospecting* by Jeb Blount (Wiley, 2015), *Combo Prospecting* by Tony J. Hughes (AMACOM, 2018) and *Problem Prospecting* by Ackers et al (independently published, 2020).

The simple fact is though that if you don't get through to the right prospects, your chances of doing any business with them are slim to zero, so the initial engagement is a critical part of the sales process. Whether you are directly responsible for prospecting, or collaborate with others to gain access to prospects, if you are to sell transformationally, then the prospecting activity needs to be aligned to these principles.

The number one mistake many prospectors make, whether messaging, emailing or making the call, is failing to understand this basic rule: if you want to engage in conversation with someone, you need to start with a topic that is of interest to them. It is unlikely that you, your product or your company is going to be the trigger and yet we see so often an email or message that starts with: "I'd like to introduce our company."

Or a phone call that start with: "If you've got a minute, I'd like to introduce myself and let you know about…"

This approach might occasionally work, after all a broken clock is still right twice a day, but you have to make a lot of calls and send out countless emails to get any sort of hit rate. When sellers focus on quantity rather than quality of activity, as a result of the long hours worked and high levels of rejection, they are likely to suffer from burn-out and loss of motivation.

This becomes a downward spiral and is one of the main reasons why many sellers stop picking up the phone and revert to 'Comfort Zone' selling. They end up contacting and seeing the same people repeatedly, and they fail to expand their network both within their existing accounts and in time spent prospecting for new business.

In the New World, this is a dangerous strategy. Those existing accounts that helped sellers to achieve their annual targets are likely to be fewer, and decisions regarding how a company spends its budget will require even more stringent sign-off processes. If your business has a growth plan, it will be extremely difficult to achieve that plan if you are solely reliant on your existing customers to keep spending.

Planning and Preparation

If you are going to focus on the quality of your prospecting outreach, then starting a more personalised conversation with your prospect (as opposed to generally just pitching what you do) will require planning and research.

Sales people, with a few honourable exceptions, aren't always the greatest planners. Planners tend to go into professions such as finance, project management or operations. The Transformational Seller needs to be more strategic and plan their approach.

With many prospectors under pressure to meet KPIs, their first aim is often to 'get the meeting', regardless of any strong qualification. Note, the problem goes back to the short-term horizon of the prospector being just the achievement of a meeting.

In activity-based roles, planning and preparation tend to be the first things that get neglected (perhaps because the Comfort Zone seller is also spending two days putting together a proposal before gaining any client commitment!).

The Transformational Seller plans their approach more methodically. They will target the right clients and stakeholders and start the conversation with something potentially compelling.

To assist you with this approach, you can utilise a PESTLE (political, economic, social, technological, legal, environmental) analysis to review what's happening in your prospect's world. Understanding how the various PESTLE factors might be affecting your prospect's business, and linking these back to your offering, you can open up a conversation with meaningful and relevant dialogue. By segmenting and targeting your prospecting activity around particular disciplines and industries, your knowledge base increases with each prospecting conversation you have.

In addition to the PESTLE approach, you should research the individual and company you are prospecting: including the 'news' section on their website, recent tweets or LinkedIn posts. This will help you find a 'hook' for opening the conversation and gaining some traction, particularly if there's some form of connection between you or your businesses that you can reference. The more you can tailor and personalise your opening, the greater the chance of engagement.

Starting the Conversation

So many introductions are bland and insipid, or simply too 'salesy', aggressive, transactional and put the prospect off.

The Transformational Seller, irrespective of whether they write an email, a social media post, or make a phone call, needs to start the conversation the way it should continue by:

- focusing on outcomes;
- leveraging expertise;
- fostering collaboration.

Look at the following examples taken from real-life cold outreach approaches; email, LinkedIn message and cold calls that we have seen and received and see how they match up. (We have changed the names and details to protect identity.)

Cold call introduction

Hi Steve – It's Jenny Stevens here from DataXY.

How are you today?

Here at DataXY we focus on cyber security and I'm calling as I'd like to get a meeting with you to discuss your company's security policy.

Email introduction

From: Jack Matthews
Subject: Employee Engagement

Hi Bryn

I've tried to make contact a couple of times to see if you are interested in our new app that uses short-burst exercise programmes for employees. I would love to get a call in your diary to let you know more and share with you its effectiveness in reversing the impact of sedentary desk work.

If you're interested, let me know...

LinkedIn message

Hi Steve

At ABC we are a training solutions company that specialises in comprehensive LMS, eLearning, training videos and customised ILT. It would be great to speak with you about how we could help you and your business in the current climate.

Reviewing these three approaches, we see very little that ties into the three pillars of Transformational Selling:

Outcomes – the email comes closest to achieving this with "reversing the impact of sedentary work", which alludes to a potential outcome.

Expertise – the LinkedIn message is the closest to hinting at this through "specialises in".

Collaboration – the cold caller mentions having a discussion so in these terms it is the closest to the collaboration target.

Let's see how each could be improved. Firstly, the cold caller.

Cold call introduction

Hi – It's Jenny Stevens here from DataXY.

I believe you know Jeff Peters?

I was given your name by Jeff who suggested you are a good person to speak to.

I've been working with him to secure his network and prevent any data losses as a result of the major shift that he, and a lot of our clients, have seen towards remote working.

It would be great to get a few minutes with you to understand more about how you are responding to this and to share ideas around how we have seen other organisations meet this challenge...

"I believe you know Jeff Peters" uses a referral of somebody the prospect knows.

"...you are a good person to speak to" with an emphasis on the 'you' demonstrates a connection.

"...have seen towards remote working" uses the social/technological change within the PESTLE framework.

"Working with him to secure his network and prevent data losses..." refers to **outcomes.**

"Understand more... share ideas..." hints at proposed **collaboration**.

"How we have seen other organisations..." is starting to leverage **expertise**.

Secondly, the email.

Email introduction

From: Jack Matthews
Subject: Working conditions impacting productivity?

Hi Bryn

I see that you have recently expanded your inside sales team.

One of the challenges that many businesses face is retaining high levels of employee productivity, particularly in sedentary desk jobs.

At XYZ, I talk to a lot of business leaders who are looking to improve the productivity and effectiveness of their teams and would be keen to understand how you are currently promoting well-being and its impact on your productivity.

We have some interesting findings to share with you.

"I see that you have recently…" makes the recipient feel that this is a personal message.

"…sedentary desk jobs" refers to social and potential environmental elements of the PESTLE and makes it relevant.

"Improve the productivity and effectiveness…" focuses on **outcomes**.

"One of the challenges for many businesses…" highlights a recognised problem that the customer may be aware of and demonstrates **expertise**.

"…keen to understand… share with you" are all part of fostering **collaboration**.

LinkedIn message

Hi Steve

How do you maximise the impact that skills development has on your business results?

As an L&D professional, it would be great to get your thoughts on this and how technology can support you.

I have some observations from clients that we are currently working with at ABC that I would be happy to share with you.

Would you be open to discussing?

"As an L&D professional…" demonstrates that they know and understand who Steve is and his role.

"…how technology can support…" is the T in the PESTLE analysis.

"Maximise impact… on business results" starts with **outcomes**.

"I have some observations from clients…" suggests the **expertise** that they can bring to the conversation.

"…open to discussing…" and "…happy to share with you" suggests **collaboration**.

STAGE 4 – REFINE

There's no magic bullet to use when prospecting. Sometimes a prospect responds to the first contact you make, others never engage. It's about persistence and activity. Most importantly, it's about learning.

Over time, experimenting with different interactions and cadences will help you to spot the patterns which increase your success rate. We frequently see people repeating the same things, slogging hard yet achieving poor results. Their response is to work harder and make more calls, or else give up.

Prospecting is about quality and quantity of activity. It's essential that you continue to experiment with approaches, order and cadence. Discipline and structure in your approach is the only way to gather the data and information that will enable you to refine and develop your prospecting activity.

Qualification – In or Out

Qualification

Qualification is the ongoing process of understanding a sales opportunity and in particular identifying:

- How likely it is that a customer will make a purchase.
- How likely it is that the purchase will be made with you.
- What needs to happen for you to win the deal.

Ultimately qualification is the measure of effort verses reward and enables sellers to make better decisions about which opportunities they should be investing their time and effort into.

Qualifying whether opportunities are realistic is based on:

- The potential need for your product or service and ability to deliver an outcome.
- Whether you are engaging with the right person.
- The timing of engagement.
- The potential match for your business.

The best sellers we have observed qualify well and early to avoid spending too much time on opportunities that don't materialise.

During tough times, businesses often tend to operate in survival mode. In sales, this often means dealing with anyone who is, or might be, willing to give you time (in the first instance) and ultimately willing to spend. The traditional thinking is that sellers can't afford to be too choosy.

In reality this approach holds many sellers back from being successful. If your customer is only interested in the cheapest deal they can possibly get, and you are a premium supplier, then the questions to ask yourself are as follows: is it really worth getting involved? If your customer wants you to send over your best possible price before they are prepared to speak to you again, is it actually worth your time to do so?

The Transformational Seller focuses at every stage on whether or not the customer is a good fit for them and their business. It's naturally hard to walk away from sales opportunities, but these sellers are the best precisely because they have learned when to do this.

Exercise: The PESTLE Analysis

Using the PESTLE analysis identify three different external factors that could potentially be impacting your customers right now. Note that these should be factors that are relevant to your offering.

Identify the issues or problems that are likely to be causing problems for potential customers, and then work them into your outreach messaging.

CHAPTER SUMMARY

- The first stage of prospecting is to define the sweet spot including: who could benefit most from what the seller has to offer and why; who has similar challenges to the seller's existing customer base; and which organisations are going to be the best fit.
- The Transformational Seller will prioritise their prospects to identify those who they have the highest chance of success with. The seller must allocate their time and effort accordingly.
- Finding a number of potential stakeholders increases the Transformational Seller's chances of opening up the

conversation and converting the prospect into a customer.

- Research and planning are fundamental in developing a contact strategy and how to open up the conversation with clients. The balance should be between ensuring that the seller does enough research against over-investing in one prospect that doesn't materialise.
- A **PESTLE Analysis**, combined with researching individuals and companies will provide the seller with the hooks, questions and topics to open up good conversations.
- The contact strategy should include utilising all of the tools at the seller's disposal for engaging with their prospects. Social media, email and messaging are all extremely useful tools to support calling activity rather than replacing it.
- The seller's opening, whether by message or call, should look to demonstrate that they have a connection or a reason to engage which links to the three core pillars of Transformational Selling: **focus on outcomes**; **leverage expertise** and **foster collaboration**.
- Refining the process means continually assessing and reviewing the numbers, identifying what's working and what could be improved, and then making the necessary changes.

CHAPTER 7

THE POWER OF COLLABORATIVE DISCOVERY (THE SCOPE MODEL)

Discovery consists of seeing what everybody has seen,

and thinking what nobody has thought.

Albert Szent-Gyorgyi

THE SCOPE MODEL

Discover, or discovery, is often cited as being one of the most persuasive words in the English language, and it's easy to see why. When we think of 'discovery' we think of exploring new lands, breakthroughs in science and the creation of new opportunities.

Discover is also the most important word in Transformational Selling.

If the Transformational Sales approach was a car, then the Discovery Phase would be the engine. This is the phase where the deal can be won or lost, where the opportunity grows or dies and where the seller can differentiate their offering and build value in their solution without even talking about it.

In Chapter 3, we recognised the importance of the first two phases of the customer buying journey, **initial interest** and **establishing needs**, in shaping both the desire and key decision-making criteria for the customer. The Discovery Phase needs to facilitate the customer through these critical stages.

In essence the objectives for the Transformational Seller in the Discovery Phase are to:

- Define the customer's required outcomes, their actual needs and create a compelling reason for the customer to continue on their buying journey.
- Influence and guide the customer's thinking around the key criteria and requirements for a potential solution.
- Conduct effective qualification of the opportunity.
- Establish credibility as 'the expert' by creating some visionary moments for the client.
- Test out the boundaries or parameters of any potential solution.
- Gain commitment to an action plan as to how to move the opportunity forward and establish, as part of the collaborative approach, which other stakeholders need to be involved in the process.

The Discovery Phase is much more than a mere fact-finding exercise. Naturally, as the seller you will be asking questions, but these are part of the process to understand the customer's thinking, their key drivers and their expected outcomes. Moreover, the questions you ask will guide your customer to elevate, in their own mind, the importance of your offering and commit to action to move the sales process forward.

If the Transformational Seller is focused on introducing change into the customer's business, then the Discovery Phase is the process of enabling the customer to understand why change is necessary and make a commitment to change.

In Chapter 1, we discussed the link between Transformational Sales and effective coaching. We made the point that both are focused on initiating and implementing change within an individual in order to achieve a positive outcome.

With this in mind, the Transformational Seller should consider what they can learn from professional coaching and apply it to their Discovery Phase.

Coaching the customer

The key lessons we can learn from coaching include:

- Focusing on outcomes and defining what success looks like for the individual.
- Avoid 'telling' the customer too much: successful coaches 'ask' instead of 'tell'.
- Encourage the customer to explore the issues and articulate them in their own words.
- Enable the customer to come up with the right ideas themselves: people have a much greater degree of ownership for ideas that they have generated.

This final point is critical: the more involved the customer is in exploring their issues, identifying root causes and developing solutions, the greater degree of commitment and ownership they will have to their buying journey.

THE PROBLEM WITH BYPASSING DISCOVERY

Whilst discovery is the sales engine, it often gets cut short or bypassed. This is usually down to a naivety on behalf of the seller, a lack of confidence or a lack of patience.

The Discovery Bypass

Imagine the following scenario (and this is one that we've observed many times).

The prospect has a problem. It is one they want to get resolved quickly, so they reach out to you to see what you can offer. They seem to have a good handle on what the problem is and what they need in order to fix it. In the interests of moving forward quickly, they ask if you can put together a proposal quotation that they can take to their board.

The board meeting is imminent and, with the end of your sales quarter coming up, you see this as a potentially quick win. You produce a proposal and send it to the client in time to present it.

You speak a couple of days later and, unfortunately, they have decided not to proceed. Instead, they have opted to implement an internal solution as a short-term fix, or alternatively they have gone with a cheaper competitor offering, or a company that they had used previously.

Sound familiar?

The problem was created when the Discovery Phase was bypassed in order to speed up the process. During this phase, the issue could have been explored in more detail alongside the compelling events that were driving this.

The seller could have investigated the alternative options and competitor offerings that were being considered, reviewed the client's perception of the pros and cons of each potential solution, and looked to influence their wish list. They could have questioned further about the Board and how much of a priority this was likely to be for them, who they felt was most and least in favour and what objections might arise.

They could also have reviewed what other issues or challenges the customer might foresee in gaining agreement and worked on enabling their contact to manage these situations, or better still, worked on a strategy to directly influence the board and its members.

The Discovery Phase is so much more than a case of asking what the problem is so you can present a way to fix it. This is your opportunity to uncover how big the problem really is (verses the client's perception of how big they currently view it), what other problems exist that they haven't seen, and, armed with this information, plan your strategy and approach accordingly.

If your sales pipeline and opportunities are stalling or failing to convert, in our experience, it is generally because you haven't conducted an effective discovery.

COLLABORATIVE DISCOVERY

The concept of conducting discovery within the sales process is not new. Therefore, it's disheartening how often when we meet a client for the first time, and they ask us at the outset whether we need to connect to the screen. Perhaps they are not wishing to make any assumptions, but it does beg the question how often they and their teams meet with potential vendors for the first time and start the process by sharing a slide deck.

We know from working with many clients about the large number of sellers who still have the tendency to 'show up and throw up'. In other words, they are very quick to get into running a demonstration, producing literature or showcasing their products and services. We've conducted many sales simulations and assessments of sellers where we have given them just twenty minutes to conduct the Discovery Phase – nowhere near enough time to do it justice considering the potential complexity of their offering – and yet they still run out of questions in half the allotted time!

One challenge in getting sellers to conduct an effective discovery meeting has been the sellers' reluctance or lack of skill in asking questions. This is generally a reflection of their confidence to ask the right questions and their reluctance to relinquish control of the conversation, even though it is the person who asks the questions who maintains control.

This is also symptomatic of a lack of structure. Any organisation can give their sales team a list of ten, twenty, or even fifty questions to ask as part of a discovery meeting. However, it's not as simple as working your way through a list; that approach can help sellers to gather information, but it doesn't enable them to guide their customer towards a conclusion.

Successful coaches use their questions to keep their 'coachee' on topic, get them talking and enable them to realise the way forward for themselves. The successful coach knows how to ask questions but doesn't necessarily know what questions they will be asking from the outset. Instead, they focus on exploring one topic at a time, providing just enough input to keep the conversation moving in the right direction.

The coaching models that they use typically follow a similar tried-and-tested format that moves their coachee through a process of reflection, generation of ideas and a commitment to action. The Transformational Seller uses the Discovery Phase to move their customer through a similar process.

In taking the best coaching models that exist and applying these principles to the sales process, we have developed the following key phases that enable the Transformational Seller to **SCOPE** the opportunity.

The **SCOPE** Model provides a framework for the discovery conversation together with the critical milestones that should be achieved along the way.

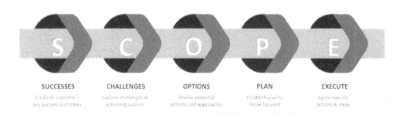

SUCCESSES	CHALLENGES	OPTIONS	PLAN	EXECUTE
Establish customer's key success outcomes	Explore challenges in achieving success	Review potential options and approaches	Establish plan to move forward	Agree specific actions & steps

Figure 7.1: The SCOPE Model for Discovery

IMPLEMENTING THE SCOPE MODEL

"Would you tell me, please, which way I ought to go from here?"

"That depends a good deal on where you want to get to," said the Cat.

"I don't much care where—" said Alice.

"Then it doesn't matter which way you go," said the Cat.

Alice in Wonderland, Lewis Carrol

When meeting with a customer (virtually or in person) there is usually some 'housekeeping' to be handled first which involves introductions, rapport building, review of agenda and objectives. Once done, it's vital that the Transformational Seller takes control and utilises questions to engage the customer. The agenda should aim to mirror the SCOPE Model that we will be making use of during the Discovery Phase.

SUCCESSES – ESTABLISH THE CUSTOMER'S KEY SUCCESS OUTCOMES

We kick off here with the first element: **Successes**. As Stephen Covey pointed out in his best-selling text *The 7 Habits of Highly Effective People*, "Start with the end in mind." This is the sentiment that the Cheshire Cat expresses to Alice.

The buying journey is an emotional one and starting with positivity will help drive the conversation forward. It's not the only emotion that the customer will experience during discovery, but it serves our purpose that this should be the starting point. You can only collaborate with someone if you have a shared vision of the outcomes that need to be achieved.

The success criteria define the customer's 'why'. In other words, the reasons why they focus their efforts this way. They will be driven by achieving the success criteria: it's how they get paid and bonused; how their performance is assessed; how they keep their job; and how they get promoted or fired.

The success criteria provide an 'anchor' for the ongoing sales conversation, something that the seller can go back to throughout the process as a reminder of why they are having the conversation and what they and the customer are jointly trying to achieve. There may be points where the conversation gets tough, where the customer raises reservations, where they have to restate the value or where they need to get the customer to commit to decisive action. In each case they revert to the success criteria – the outcomes – as a place to regather and regroup their thoughts.

In terms of assessing the customer's success criteria the seller needs to be clear in establishing the following:

- The specific measures for success that the customer is looking to achieve.
- The qualitative and quantitative objectives against which performance will be measured.
- The objectives the customer has been set and those that they have set for themselves.
- How these objectives and outcomes fit with the business' broader goals and targets, to ascertain the strategic importance of them.
- How the different stakeholders' outcomes may conflict, and how they can be better aligned.
- The potential rewards and consequences for achieving or failing to achieve objectives and outcomes.
- How the customer intends to go about achieving these objectives and the strategies and tactics they intend to use.

The aim is to encourage your customer to elaborate on the success that they are looking to achieve and why it is important. As they continue to talk about their success criteria, so their level of interest increases. The more they can picture their successes, the more you can get them to feel and taste it, the more engaged they will become in the conversation.

Chapter 2 referred to the concept of the value chain and the idea that the product is linked through a sequence of events to the overall goals and outcomes for the customer. You may need to direct your questioning towards a particular aspect of the customer's business in order to ensure that the success criteria and outcomes that you focus on at this stage are aligned to your offering.

One of the key attributes of the Transformational Seller is their ability to recognise their offering on the value chain and establish a route between their value proposition (what's different about their offering and the size of the problem it solves) and the ultimate outcome for their customer.

It may be that you are not speaking to the right person, either because you are engaging with someone who is not concerned with the strategies and outcomes or that they are in the wrong area of the business. We once engaged with a company that specialised in providing financial software, only to find that their sales team were primarily prospecting IT managers. Once they switched their approach to targeting finance directors, whose lives were made easier by their product, they found they gained significantly greater traction.

Whilst the discussion around the customer's success criteria should invoke general feelings of positivity and motivation, it may also create a tinge of concern. The realisation that these objectives or targets may not be achieved, that there's a lot of work to do or that there are risk factors that sit outside of the customer's control which can impact their success, may weigh heavily on the customer's mind. This links to the next phase of the SCOPE conversation: **challenges**.

CHALLENGES – EXPLORE CHALLENGES IN ACHIEVING SUCCESS

In Chapter 3 it was established that the customer buying journey is an emotional one. Having worked through the customer's success criteria, established what is truly important to them and understood their motivations, the Transformational Seller can now change the direction of the conversation and lead them through a more emotionally taxing phase.

When it comes to challenges, you want the customer to explore the potential issues and problems that may thwart efforts to achieve success. These may be in clear view of the customer, or conversely, they may be hidden or not yet recognised as a problem (remember Henry Ford and his 'faster horse').

The aim is to use questioning to encourage the customer to work through where and what the potential issues are in achieving the success criteria. A good place to start is by asking: "What could get in the way of you achieving X?"

Typically, these challenges will come from a number of sources that might include both internal issues such as a lack of resources or budget, skills or capabilities or external factors such as economic conditions, competitive landscape or regulatory pressures.

You need to encourage the conversation to explore:

- These challenges in detail and any plans the customer might have to mitigate them.
- Your experiences of having encountered these problems before.
- The impact that these issues could have on the customer's ability to achieve their objectives.
- Any knock-on effect or consequences as a result.

You should also use your expertise to introduce additional areas of challenge or concern for the customer. These may relate to changes or observations from the external environment (PESTLE criteria) or knowledge of other clients who have experienced similar challenges.

As with the **Success** stage of the SCOPE conversation, whilst the discussions on **Challenges** can start off broadly, you will need to hone the conversation towards those particular challenges that your offering can either directly solve or mitigate against, or that can be offset by your offering. This requires you to have a good understanding of your place in the value chain.

By zoning in on these specific challenges and the potential impact that you could have on the customer achieving their goals, you are aiming to create a **success-challenges gap**.

This gap is the distance between the success the customer is striving to achieve and where they actually might end up. The greater the widening of the gap, the stronger the need for them to plug it, so your aim as the Transformational Seller is to make the gap as wide as possible.

Summarising the Gap – Wrapping up Success and Challenges

We are now at the crucial stage of the sales process where the customer's acknowledgement of the gap and the requirement to do something will dictate whether they will commit to following their buying journey through to completion.

It is worth bearing in mind that the gap should enable the customer to recognise the need to address the issues in terms of implementing a solution to mitigate or resolve the issue and implementing the right solution to resolve the issue.

Consider the difference between the two: for some customers the need to 'buy' something may not be in question, therefore you should guide the customer towards the recognition that it is a specific aspect of your offering that the customer needs to focus on.

If the need to act was not completely apparent to the customer before this point, it should be now. In other words, the assessment of the **success-challenges gap** should cement the need for change and complete the first stages of their buying journey **initial interest** and **establish needs**.

One of our favourite questions from this stage is: "What do you need to do differently to ensure that you are able to achieve your objectives?"

We will look at questioning in more detail in the next chapter. However, this question encapsulates everything that we are working towards. It is a good question because the need for your customer to make a change is automatically in-built and places the focus on how they need to achieve this difference. It's designed to create that lightbulb moment for your customer and acts as a bridge towards the next phase of the SCOPE conversation where the options are explored.

OPTIONS – REVIEWING POTENTIAL OPTIONS AND APPROACHES

This is the part of the process when you as a seller might start to get excited. It could be the stage when you finally get to talk about your offering and can spout forth with all of your polished enthusiasm as you walk your customer through your well-rehearsed sales pitch.

After all, you've held back until you confirmed the customer's needs and requirements, built value in the need for a solution and demonstrated the risks and consequences of not acting. Now is your time to shine.

STOP!

Stop right now!

Now is not the time for your pitch. This needs to be crafted around key win themes, it needs to build on the information you have gathered and, even more importantly, it needs to be tailored to different stakeholders who will be involved in making the decision.

During **options** stage, the Transformational Seller should:

1. Encourage their customer to continue to talk.

2. Guide their customer to map out, at a high level, what the solution could look like.
3. Prompt and promote discussion around key aspects of the solution that align to your offering.

The more that you can guide your customer to help create their perfect solution, the greater the buy-in will be to your offering when you come to pitching it back.

Things to note:

- Keep the discussion at a high level and base it around the principles of how any proposed solution should operate. This is about getting the customer to verbalise their most important criteria, not starting to dictate the specification.
- Ensure that the customer identifies your key differentiators as part of the **options** stage. You may need to prompt them through your questioning to ensure that these are integral to their ideal solution.
- Steer the customer away from areas that are not a critical part of the offering using questioning to focus the customer back to the most important outcomes and move them towards the aspects of your solution that achieve these.

Shepherding the customer

Steve: In many sports, the concept of 'shepherding' the opponent is a key defensive tactic. The idea is to position yourself in a way that encourages them to go in a particular direction – the one that makes it easier for you to defend. For example, this means in rugby taking advantage of the touchline; in football, making your opponent go in the direction of their weaker foot.

In the same way, shepherding your customer during the options stage towards your strengths or away from areas that don't play to your strengths is vitally important.

For example, we have had clients who have requested that we bring in professional actors to play the part of a prospective customer for sales simulation exercises during training programmes, having seen this approach used in the past.

We are resistant to this idea because: it's expensive; it creates a lot of additional work; and, however thorough the briefing, actors are unlikely to be able to answer detailed or technical questions unless provided in advance. We don't believe that it adds value.

In such circumstances we have to 'shepherd' the customer away from this idea through reviewing the key outcomes they need from the programme. For example, take a customer who wants to achieve "ten percent growth in revenue through greater conversion of sales opportunities".

Then you need to find the answers to the following:

- What the key takeaways they would need to gain from these training exercises to enable the outcome to be achieved?
- How important it would be to have someone who can answer their questions realistically to simulate an actual customer?
- How valuable it would be to get insightful feedback from the person playing the customer?

Next, we can ask the customer to assess whether an actor is going to be able to offer insightful feedback at a discovery meeting around, say, a workflow software solution.

We can then suggest alternatives including using their own leaders to play the customer (it's always great to get leaders involved in the coaching process) or, as we have done on occasions, got some of their own customers to take part (now there's an example of true collaboration!).

The overarching theme of this stage is to create an outline of the customer's ideal solution: one that is suitably aligned to your offering in advance of creating and delivering your proposal. In other words, aligning the customer's wish list in Step 2 of the customer buying journey (**establish needs**) to your potential offering.

PLAN – ESTABLISH PLAN TO MOVE FORWARD

One of the greatest barriers to planning is the horizons that restrict our ability to see beyond a certain point. For young children, the horizon isn't much further away than the next mealtime. As they get older, it becomes birthdays, Christmas or the end of a school term. For parents it can be frustrating trying to get their children to see the value of eating healthily or doing their homework, when the benefits of doing so stretch way beyond their natural horizons.

The same principle applies to sellers and to customers alike. Sellers are often afflicted by a misalignment of their **event horizon** with their customer's. Frequently, the seller's event horizon is based around the point where the sale is complete, whereas for the customer it is when the sale delivers the eventual outcome, which may be a less clearly defined point in the future.

For example, if the customer's primary focus is to increase productivity, the questions to ask are: at what point does your offering deliver this? Is it when they sign up, when they first start using the product or service, or after two years? How much does productivity need to increase before they feel that they have really benefitted? Is it when they see a one percent, ten percent or twenty percent improvement that it feels worthwhile?

Creating **urgency to act** is one of the greatest challenges for any seller. In the New World, we fully expect that decision making within organisations will be more laborious. This will be due to the following:

- Reduced individual decision-making autonomy.
- Increasing influence of professional procurement functions.
- Tightened and heavily scrutinised budgets.
- Greater risk aversion.

Therefore, the planning stage is critical for the Transformational Seller to gain momentum and create the urgency to act. The recommended approach is to create a 'backward plan' with the customer's input and – starting with the end in mind – to agree on a specific date (or timescale) for when success will have been achieved and measured. Then you can work backwards to identify the key milestones along the way.

The mistake that many sellers make is to regard the sale date (the date when the sale is confirmed, the order is placed or even delivered) as the end date for this process, when in the customer's mind this is just one of many milestones that need to be completed.

Confirming a date for when the customer should see results makes the outcome and benefits muchmore tangible. This can be leveraged against key dates such as year-end or the next board meeting rather than your key dates (e.g., end of your quarter).

In working backwards, you need to agree the timescales for implementation and embedding, allow for lead times and therefore agree on a potential sign-off date. Next, you can work with your customer to map out the process in terms of: who will need to get involved; what steps need to happen in terms of securing an agreement; key decision-making milestones (present to the team, the board etc); the procurement process and lead times.

This may feel like we're jumping the gun by mapping out the critical steps of the sale and the implementation of the sales process before we have even pitched our solution. However, this planning is on the assumption that we are able to present a solution that meets the customer's needs and delivers confidence that we can enable them to achieve their desired outcomes.

The great thing about mapping out the process at this stage is that it enables us to:

- **Evaluate the strength of the opportunity** – the more committed the customer is to working through the plan, the more engaged they will therefore become. This supports forecasting as we start to get an idea of the complexity and length of the decision-making process.
- **Open up the discussion around who needs to be involved** – it's very useful to get insight into which stakeholders will be involved and what buttons you may need to press for each of them. Do this before your start to prepare a formal pitch or presentation for the business.
- **'Future Pace' the opportunity** – this means putting the customer beyond the point where they have made a decision. In their own mind, they have worked through the go/no-go barrier and they have started to consider life on the other side. You have planted the seed that it's a case of 'when' not 'if' you are able to produce a proposal that they are happy to sponsor within the business.

The production of the plan, which may be relatively loose at this stage, naturally leads to the final stage of the SCOPE discovery process – the execution.

EXECUTION – THE PIVOTAL PHASE

We can now summarise where you should now be within the discovery process with the customer.

Success	You've established their key success criteria: the outcomes they are trying to achieve and how these are aligned to the goals and strategies of the business.
Challenges	The customer has opened up regarding potential challenges that could prevent them from achieving these goals and the potential implications.
(The Gap)	They have acknowledged the gap between where they are aiming to be and where they are right now (thus completing/reinforcing the first stage of their buying journey – **initial interest**).
Options	The customer has identified what the critical factors are for implementing a solution which incorporates the key differentiators and selling points around your potential solution (Stage 2 of their buying Journey – **establishing needs**).
Plan	You have jointly walked through the backward plan and identified key milestones.

The final stage is to start work on the implementation of this plan and agree what the next steps are for both of you. This part of the plan is pivotal.

Was it really a good sales meeting?

We've heard too many conversations that go something like this:

"How did that meeting go?"

"Great. There's definitely a decent opportunity there. The customer has a need and really liked my suggestions. It could be quite a sizeable piece of business."

"Sounds good, what are the next steps?"

"I'm going to send through a proposal for them to review, outlining what we can do."

"Ok, and what have they specifically committed to doing?"

"Well ... nothing at this stage."

However well you might feel that the conversation went, without gaining active commitment* from the customer then you have failed to establish anything concrete from the discovery meeting.

*Active Commitment

Active Commitment is where the customer agrees to make a firm commitment to investing their and time and potentially other resources into the next step of the process.

Active Commitment is in stark contrast to Passive Commitment where it is only the seller who has to commit time and resource into the next step.

A positive result would include the following examples. The customer has agreed to do the following:

- Send through some further information (metrics/stats etc) which you can use to prepare your proposal.

- Engage and gather information from other key stakeholders.
- Set up an introduction to other key stakeholders to join the next call or meeting.
- Invite you to an internal meeting or call, or even visit your premises.
- Agreed a specific time and date for a call/meeting for you to present your proposal.

What is striking about this list? It is that the customer is also now doing a lot of the work, not just you. If that is the case, then you are doing the right things to move the opportunity forward.

The more your customer has to do, the greater the degree of equity they have in the process and the greater the chance of the sales progressing beyond the next stage.

You agreeing to pour hours of effort into producing a proposal or quotation shows commitment, but you need something in return, such as a specific time for you present it and bring it to life, particularly if that were to include other stakeholders and decision makers.

The main thing to remember is that as an expert, you are establishing a relationship with your customer that is not subservient, it's a partnership. It's a collaborative relationship, therefore, even at this early stage, there needs to be a degree of quid pro quo. The level of **active commitment** is one of the greatest indicators of the potential of a sales opportunity.

The next chapter looks more closely at the indicators of how to assess the potential of a sales opportunity, the process we call **qualification**. The greatest mistake we see is devoting too much time and effort to unrealistic sales opportunities or failing to develop a strategy to win the business when it is a genuine opportunity.

Exercise: SCOPE in Practice

Using SCOPE in practice, either for a customer you have recently sold to or one you are in the process of selling to, answer the following:

- What are their key success criteria?
- What are they trying to achieve and how do they measure the outcomes?
- What are the challenges to them achieving these outcomes? What questions can you ask to establish and potentially widen the gap between the **S** and the **C**?
- What options have you discussed with them (with respect to your offering)? What alternative options do they have available to them?
- Construct a backward plan based on what you know about their buying process, the stakeholders involved, their stage within the buying journey etc. What else do you need to know in order to complete the backward plan?
- What are the next steps? How **active** is the customer's **commitment** to the next stage?

CHAPTER SUMMARY

- The Discovery Phase is arguably the most important event for the Transformational Seller. It's where they are able to guide and facilitate their customer through the first two stages of their buying journey, cementing their **initial interest** and helping them to shape and **establish needs**.
- Discovery is about questioning not only to gather information but to direct and influence the customer's thinking around their need for a solution. The process of asking questions enables the seller to control the conversation.

- Good discovery follows similar principles to coaching in that it should encourage the customer to reflect, to consider different ideas and make a commitment to moving forward.
- The SCOPE Model provides an effective structure for conducting meaningful discovery. It focuses on:

1. The customer's **success** criteria and what they are aiming to achieve.
2. The **challenges** in achieving their desired outcomes – the things that are getting in the way or might get in the way of them reaching their goals.
3. Opening up different **options** and shaping ideas around what a potential solution could look like.
4. Creating a **plan** in collaborating with the customer as to how best to proceed.
5. Agreeing a set of actions that both parties need to **execute** to move forward.

- The success of a discovery meeting is defined by the level of **active commitment** from the customer.

CHAPTER 8
QUALIFICATION FOR THE TRANSFORMATIONAL SELLER

The pessimist complains about the wind;

the optimist expects it to change;

the realist adjusts the sails.

William Arthur Ward

Happy ears versus keeping it real

Steve: The first time we came across the term 'happy ears' it came from a client frustrated at the number of sales stuck in the later stages of their pipeline.

Forecasting is critical for a manufacturing company. The ability to predict accurately production levels and organise materials, shift patterns and labour requirements has a huge impact on profitability. Over-ordering materials and having them sitting in their warehouse indefinitely is extremely costly as is bringing in contract labour for last-minute jobs. In fact, whilst the margin achieved is important, accurate forecasting is a greater factor for overall profitability.

In this particular case, the sales team were hopelessly optimistic, progressing opportunities through the pipeline stages too quickly, predicting sign-off dates too soon and over-estimating their chances of winning. Occasionally deals would linger in the early stage, with little traction. Then they would suddenly convert, which also created problems.

The business planning and profitability of the company were at the mercy of the sales team's gut instinct, and these optimistic appraisals were often based on sellers hearing what they wanted to hear – hence the term: 'happy ears'.

A customer saying that they are interested in your offering may seem positive, but if they don't have the money to buy, approval to make the decision, or a compelling case to influence those that do, then irrespective of their interest (assuming it's real and they aren't just being polite), this is not an opportunity.

Poor forecasting isn't just an issue for the planning and operations of a business, it's symptomatic of a broader problem. If there's a lack of certainty over what's happening with deals, no clear visibility or understanding of the customer's decision-making process, then how can sellers have any control or influence over what's happening?

THE QUESTIONS THAT QUALIFICATION SHOULD ANSWER

Qualification is the process of gathering intelligence around an opportunity that enables you to critically assess it and act accordingly. In essence qualification enables you to answer the following questions with an increasing degree of certainty:

- What stage is the customer at in their buying journey?
- How likely will they do something and what's the likelihood of it being with you?

- What has to happen in order for the sale to go through?
- How significant is this opportunity in the short term and in the longer term?

The degree of confidence with which you can answer these questions will enable you to make better informed decisions throughout. These informed decisions will include:

- How do we win the deal; what strategies and tactics should we employ and what should our next steps be?
- How much time and resource should we commit to this opportunity and why should we prioritise it over other opportunities?
- Should we continue to work on this opportunity, or should we bow out before we spend too much time and effort on a lost cause?

This last point may sound counter-intuitive to many organisations. Afterall, shouldn't the mindset be to go after every deal? Actually, the most successful sellers – in the words of Kenny Rodgers' song *The Gambler,* "know when to hold 'em, know when to fold 'em, know when to walk away".

Qualification is not an absolute term. Even though organisations refer to opportunities as being qualified or unqualified, the reality is that a sale is never fully qualified until it is won or lost. Even then, the reasons why it was won or lost may not be fully understood.

In the New World, technology is increasingly enabling sellers to make better decisions around which opportunities to pursue and how best to pursue them. However, this will still depend upon accurate information being captured at an early stage in the process.

A system is only ever as good as the quality of information input: GIGO – Garbage In, Garbage Out!

QUALIFICATION: THE TWO-TIER APPROACH OF BANT AND CASE

To support sellers, a number of qualification structures and frameworks have been developed and adapted. Examples include MEDDICC, BANT and SCOTSMAN. These frameworks have a simple mnemonic as a memory aid or sense check for the seller as they go through their qualification process.

As with all of these tools and frameworks, the devil is in the detail, but they do have genuine practical benefits for sellers and sales leaders.

The problems we have seen with their adoption is not the frameworks themselves, but how they are applied. When they form part of a review process to analyse deals in progress and highlight the knowns and unknowns, they can be highly effective. If they are used as a structure or a script for the sale, they are likely to be problematic and deliver a poor experience for the customer.

In multi-stage sales processes, which require a Transformational approach, the qualification can be split into two tiers. These tiers focus on two different questions. The first focuses on understanding whether there even is a real opportunity here; the second considers driving the strategy and tactics needed to win it.

TIER 1 QUALIFICATION – BANT

Figure 8.1: Tier 1 - BANT Qualification Methodology

Perhaps the most well-known and widely adopted qualification process is BANT. This straightforward framework covers many of the basics of qualification:

- Budget – the budget and budgeting process assigned for this project.
- Authority – who is involved in the decision-making process.
- Need – how great the customer's need is and what is driving that need.
- Timescales – what timescales they are working towards and the events that are driving them.

Sellers, particularly those operating transactionally, will often see these criteria as merely a tick box exercise or as a list of questions to ask e.g., "Do they have a budget?" The Transformational Seller seeks to go much deeper under each heading.

Budget

It's not just a case of whether the customer has a budget assigned and, if so, how much. The Transformational Seller is also concerned with issues such as:

- How budgets are typically allocated.
- What flexibility there is in the budget.
- Whether the budget has been ring-fenced for this project or is coming from a central pot.
- How the customer arrived at the figure, what assumptions were made and what research went into identifying the budget.
- Who the budget holder is/which department holds the budget.
- What the approval process looks like and the limits of authority across different decision makers.

In times of uncertainty the allocation processes become much tighter, involve more checks and balances and can be an ever-moving target. Your key contacts may not even be sure of the budget process until they have tried to secure funds.

Authority

It is unlikely that there will be one ultimate decision maker, but instead purchase decisions will require consensus from a DMU.

Within this group of stakeholders, there will be varying degrees of influence exerted and different roles assigned. Some will look at the decision from a technical or financial perspective, others from a more strategic or functional standpoint. Some will have a vested interest as it's their specific challenges you are proposing to solve, whilst those removed from the day-to-day issues associated with your offering will take a more dispas-sionate view.

Whilst we refer to the DMU as a Decision-Making *Unit*, the Transformational Seller recognises that there is not necessarily a high degree of unity across this group. All those involved are likely to have different agendas for their wish list, assign different priorities and may even have conflicting criteria against which they will be judging and evaluating your offering.

In qualifying each opportunity, the Transformational Seller is looking for an understanding of:

- The different individuals and groups likely to be involved within the decision.
- The relative influence that each individual or group will have over the decision-making process.
- The different 'interest' that each is likely to have in the purchasing decision.
- The format and process by which the decision will be made.

Needs

With the aim of delivering desired outcomes, the key question is: what does the customer need to deliver their outcomes?

When assessing needs, sellers tend to focus purely on the specifications needed to fulfil the customer's stated requirements (e.g., the number of users, anticipated load, physical dimensions etc).

The technical specification can be open to discussion. As a Transformational Seller you may need to support, or even debate with your customer over defining the specification, reviewing and shaping it in line with the outcomes that they desire.

In terms of strategic needs, it is important to establish what is driving the customer on their buying journey. In particular, gaining clarity around the **compelling event** or the **erosion of satisfaction** that has sparked their **initial interest**, the main issues that they are looking for the solution to overcome and the potential consequences if the need is not properly addressed.

We should go a step further in analysing the extent to which the customer recognises the need and how well they understand it. If we think back to the example of the customer who thought they wanted a drill (but really needed a Kindle), it's too easy to focus solely on the specification of the drill and the size of the holes that the customer wants to create rather than the actual outcome that the customer is striving for.

Timescales

Timescales refers to the ideal timeline that the customer is working towards and the key milestones within the decision-making process. As we have noted, the Transformational Seller's timescales are built around when the customer will see the outcomes, rather than the purchase date itself, and they will work backwards from there.

Having identified a timetable of events, the focus is on the critical path to success. This is the sequence of events and anticipated timescales that represent the most direct path to the customer's outcomes. It should include lead times for delivery and installation, implementation, time for employee training and skills development to master the new system or process, and the time lag between effective deployment and use of this and the measurement of results.

The Transformational Approach to BANT

The Transformational Seller explores these areas in much greater detail than their Transactional or Consultative counterparts. They also differ in how they treat the information gathered.

For example, we have seen debates rage as to whether you should pursue an opportunity if the customer doesn't have an allocated budget. Some take the pragmatic view of establishing this at an early stage in the sales process and if the customer has not secured a budget, then it's time to move on. The counter argument is that if the need can be established and built sufficiently, the customer can sometimes then find the budget to make it happen.

Watching the endless 'toing and froing' of one particular online debate and the conviction of both parties as to their own position, it was abundantly clear that they were both spectacularly right and wrong at the same time.

If you're operating in a very transactional market, your targets are short term and it's a low-value, high-volume sale, you're going to play the odds. If the customer hasn't got the money, you are unlikely to close a deal in the short term. Transactional Sellers are generally more interested in the short term.

The Transformational Seller knows that their sales opportunities don't always involve a quick turnaround and are much more likely to play the long game. It is for this reason that they have to qualify their opportunities carefully. They will work on sales opportunities that won't necessarily close this target cycle (be that the month or the quarter), collaborating with their customers on developing the business case that requires a budget to be created.

They view authority in much the same way, recognising that purchasing decisions on the Transformational end of the spectrum are rarely made by one individual. They are less concerned with the question, "Am I speaking to the decision maker?" and more interested in, "What role does this person play within the decision-making process?", "Who else do I need to be engaging with?", "How do I get introduced?" and

"What role do I want this individual to play in supporting me through the process: information provider, introducer, technical specialist, sponsor or coach?"

TIER 2 QUALIFICATION – CASE

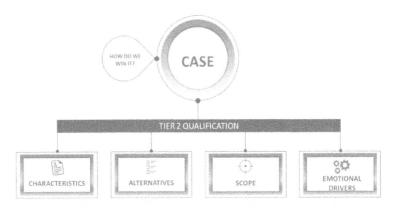

Figure 8.2: Tier 2 – CASE Qualification Methodology

The BANT qualification, when conducted thoroughly, goes a long way to answering the following questions:

- How likely is it that the customer will do something?
- What needs to happen in order for the sale to progress?

It is a useful tool for establishing how good we think the opportunity is. The significance of the compelling need, the visibility on how the decision will be made and where the customer is at regarding budget allocation are all key indicators of an opportunity's potential.

However, this tool doesn't necessarily help to develop the strategy and approach needed to *win* the opportunity. Here we need to incorporate the Tier 2 Qualification CASE. This explores:

- Characteristics
- Alternatives
- Scope
- Emotional drivers

The output of an effective CASE qualification should be the development of a series of key 'win themes'.

These will form the basis of the pitch, strategy and key messaging throughout. It enables the seller to make a compelling CASE to the client.

Characteristics

The second stage of the customer buying journey involves the customer developing a wish list: a set of characteristics that they will use to evaluate potential solutions.

Firstly, the Transformational Seller needs to establish and understand these different characteristics. If the customer is at or beyond Stage 2 of their buying journey, they will have already developed their wish list (formally or informally) and therefore the seller needs to establish the following:

- What is on the customer's wish list?
- Why are these important to them?
- What assumptions has the customer made in defining their wish list?
- How does the priority order vary between different stakeholders within the DMU?

The critical aspect here is that we are not just establishing the 'what', but also the 'why'. If certain characteristics or features are deemed important, then these are likely to have been identified through the customer's research, past history or competitor conversations.

The Transformational Seller needs to coach and guide their customer in terms of the characteristics and their relative priority on that wish list. Specifically, the seller needs to review whether the customer's priorities are correctly ordered and whether there are any obvious omissions from their wish list: areas that have been overlooked or dismissed that should be added or elevated in terms of importance. The **options** stage of the **SCOPE** Model provides the opportunity to explore this with the customer.

This stage needs to be handled carefully. You can't just tell the customer that they have got their priorities wrong. The key is in questioning, which we explore in the next chapter. Our role is to help the customer to see their priorities for themselves.

Re-prioritising your customer's wish list

Steve: Some years ago, I was looking to change my car. I spent a lot of time travelling, so my vehicle was important and I wanted it to be well equipped, comfortable and stylish. I was attracted to the German marques – BMW, Audi, Mercedes – because of the perceived quality and the image that came with a prestige brand.

However, whilst looking for showrooms with my family, we found ourselves venturing into a Volvo dealership. My perception of Volvos had always been that they were solid and reliable but premium rather than prestige. To be honest, I associated them with being middle-aged and, despite the odd grey hair, I wasn't ready for my pipe and slippers just yet.

That said, I was surprised by the stylish design, both inside and outside and impressed by the high specification, comfort and drive. The Volvo ticked a lot of boxes, but when push came to shove, it wasn't giving me the image that I wanted (emotion over logic!).

The salesman asked me for my thoughts, and I gave a positive review of the car, but he sensed in my tone and language that I was yet to be convinced.

"What else have you been looking at?" he asked.

I told him and he gave a sage nod of approval. Clearly, they were good considerations. I talked about reliability and quality, but he and I both knew that it was the brand image that I was attracted to.

At this stage, he was faced with a challenge. He could try to persuade me that the Volvo was every bit as prestigious as the other cars I had my eye on, but I was unlikely to buy into that. He could appeal to my logical side and demonstrate better value for money, but this decision wasn't about money. Sure, I had a budget, but I wasn't looking for a cheap option.

His only remaining move was to change my wish list. At this point, status and prestige were at the top of my priorities and that was a battle he was always going to struggle to win. What he needed was to introduce a new element, one that better matched both my requirements and his offering.

His next question was, "Will this car mainly be used for work or for the family?"

"Both" I replied. "I'll use it mainly during the week, but also for family trips and as a taxi service for my children!"

"OK. With that in mind, how important are the safety features in making your decision?"

That was my 'oh s**t!' moment – the point when my entire wish list altered. This was not because he told me that safety should be my number one priority – had he done so, I might have reacted very differently.

Instead, those simple questions led me to that conclusion for myself. What kind of parent doesn't put the safety of their young children at the top of their list?

He was now in a position to run through the very impressive and advanced safety features for which Volvo is renowned.

I bought it!

Alternatives

No matter how 'original' your proposition is, the customer *always* has alternatives which go beyond what many sellers see as their competitors. Ultimately you will be competing against:

- Direct Competitors – those companies who offer similar products or services to your own.
- Indirect Competitors – companies that offer a different range of products or services which provide an alternative route to achieving the customer's outcomes (this could include internal teams or solutions).
- Doing nothing – in virtually every case, one alternative is to do nothing: apathy and inaction are often your fiercest competitors.
- Other Priorities – the customer decides to put their resources (money and time) into other non-related projects. This increases in times of uncertainty or economic turmoil, as available resources become more restricted, and budgets are no longer ring-fenced for certain projects or business areas.

Uncovering the customer's alternatives is essential for the Transformational Seller, not least because considering alternatives, specifically direct competition, is an indicator as to how serious they are. Moreover, uncovering the customer's alternative options enables you to tailor your key sales message.

You need to consider:

1. If the customer's main alternative is to do nothing, then your sales argument needs to focus on the reasons for the change (**compelling event** and **erosion of satisfaction**) and the risks and issues that may continue

to hold the customer back from achieving their desired outcomes.

2. If the customer is already committed to doing something, then your argument needs to focus on what is different about your proposition and how this will ensure it delivers the right outcomes.

3. Your level of understanding of your offering. The better you understand how your offering stacks up and, more importantly differs from your competition, the stronger you will be able to emphasise these differences as you progress through the customer buying journey.

4. The customer's perception. Whilst you may have a perception of the relative strengths and weaknesses of the competitor offerings, it's the customer's perception of these that is critical to the buying decision.

It's also important that you understand how your customer views the relative differences in your offerings.

There is a line that you must be careful not to cross when it comes to discussing competitor offerings. You are unlikely to boost your credibility as the expert by criticising the competition either explicitly or through implication. However, it's often the concern around *not* crossing this line that makes many sellers back away from asking questions about competitors. They therefore miss the opportunity to develop a competitive strategy. Whilst criticising the competition is a definite no-no, it's perfectly acceptable, we would argue essential, to ask the customer the following:

- Whether they are looking at any alternatives or speaking to other suppliers.
- What their experience has been like with them.

- How they feel your proposition stacks up in comparison (both in terms of what they like and what concerns they may have).
- What they particularly liked about proposals they have seen from the competition.
- What concerns or issues they have with what they have seen from them.
- What's worked well and not so well with their current supplier.

We've encountered numerous sellers who demonstrate discomfort when asking these questions (including whether the customer is even speaking to anyone else!) Their argument is that asking about the competition is alerting your customer to the idea that they should be talking to other providers.

Let's get real here: your customers *are* aware that there are other providers and other options. If they haven't chosen to speak to anyone else at this stage, it isn't because they hadn't thought of it. The risk to asking that question is small compared with the rewards of understanding who you are competing with and gaining insight into the customer's perception of them.

Scope

As we move towards the Transformational Spectrum, strategic thinking increases, where each sale is viewed not as a one-off opportunity but as a longer-term goal to building a business relationship. The essence of this relationship is in recognising that the value goes way beyond a specific product or solving a particular problem. By demonstrating a 'bigger picture' approach, the Transformational Seller is looking at the scope to create a strong and lasting partnership. They want to enable the customer to achieve their outcomes.

Think of a patient looking to their doctor to provide pain relief for a migraine. The Transactional doctor's approach is to recommend a suitable drug to ease their patient's symptoms. The Transformational doctor looks at the root causes of the patient's migraines and recommends both short-term pain relief and a broader package to manage and ultimately prevent the symptoms.

Therefore, it is vital that the Transformational Seller qualifies and reviews the opportunity both up and downstream from where the problems occur.

By assessing the broader scope of the opportunity, the Transformational Seller can then:

- Demonstrate their expertise around the broader solution.
- Differentiate from the competition in terms of both solution and approach.
- Understand the strategic significance that this opportunity represents and allocate resources to the opportunity accordingly.

The scope may also include identifying the customer's propensity to have a more strategic relationship with you. If the customer is only willing to deal with you as a 'supplier' at arms-length, you may have to decide whether this is worth pursuing in the long run. A customer who only wants to deal with you transactionally may well abandon you for price or convenience at a later point.

Emotional Drivers

There are two things that we need to consider with emotional drivers:

- You will need to capture emotional drivers as part of your BANT and CASE analysis. This can be done directly and indirectly through your questioning.
- Emotional drivers are arguably the most important things that you should be capturing.

Research shows that emotional drivers account for eighty-four percent of the buying decision and identifying them as part of your CASE qualification is fundamental in your approach to winning the deal.

Specific focus needs to be paid to:

Success outcomes and objectives – understanding your customer's targets and objectives. It is against these measures that their performance will be judged. Their sense of achievement, rewards, recognition and career opportunities are dependent upon achieving these measures. Their greatest levels of concern and stress will be as a result of striving or failing to achieve them.

Stakeholder drivers – building a picture for the emotional drivers of all stakeholders within the decision-making process. In an ideal world you will be looking to engage with the stakeholders directly to ask such questions. However, at the very least, you should ask your current contact(s) to outline the other stakeholders' key objectives and issues as this will provide a useful starting point.

Fears, Uncertainty and Doubts (FUD) – examining the potential FUD factors that are likely to impact the customer's decision making. Remember, the greater the perceived change that you are proposing, the greater the degree of perceived risk for them.

Having identified all the different emotional drivers that are, or could be, impacting the process, you are now in a position to plan how best to manage the customer towards your required outcome, leveraging these key emotions during each conversation and interaction.

Subsequent chapters will look at techniques that can support you, including:

- Questioning techniques and approaches that will not only uncover customer emotions but also help elicit the emotional responses that will drive your customer around their buying journey.
- Weaving these emotional drivers into the core win themes of your pitch.
- Using story-telling to connect emotions to outcomes.
- Utilising core communication elements (visual, vocal, verbal) to reinforce the customer's emotional journey.

THE QUALIFICATION PROCESS (USING BANT AND CASE)

Of all the areas that we have helped businesses with, the introduction of a qualification framework has arguably been the simplest and most practical to implement and the one that potentially had the greatest positive impact on sales performance.

Our observations around qualification are as follows:

- Relatively few organisations have effectively implemented a strong qualification structure and rarely use the information gathered to make better decisions as to how or whether to progress sales opportunities.

- The qualification process is all too often treated as a tick box exercise (e.g., have they got a budget or not) rather than a sophisticated intelligence gathering one.
- The lack of effective qualification makes it difficult for sellers and sales leaders to develop their strategies and tactics for winning deals.

The Transformational Seller recognises that ongoing qualification (and re-qualification) of opportunities is the key to success. The intelligence gathered during customer interactions forms the basis of every decision they make and is carefully collated and documented.

They also recognise that BANT and CASE qualification is a result of having engaging conversations, SCOPE discovery and the continuation of questioning throughout the sales process rather than merely a check list of questions to ask.

As we move forward, we can see the importance of capturing information from the BANT and CASE qualification as part of the ongoing sales process. The introduction of more sophisticated CRM sales tools and the greater use of AI will support businesses in making better decisions around which opportunities to focus on and how best to pursue them.

However, the challenge will still be in ensuring that sellers have asked the right questions and, more importantly, listened to and understood the customer's responses.

The next chapter reviews the skills that will enable you to take your discovery process and BANT and CASE qualification to the next level through effective questioning.

This represents the most important tool in the Transformational Sellers' armoury – even more so that pitching!

See Appendix for examples of BANT and CASE qualification.

Exercise: BANT and CASE

With a blank piece of paper, write down the eight BANT and CASE headings and then list all the information relating to what you know relative to each heading.

Which headings do you have the least information on?

Where will you go to get this intelligence?

How does this help you identify the quality of the opportunity and the tactics required to win it?

CHAPTER SUMMARY

- Effective qualification should enable the Transformational Seller to gauge what stage their customer is at on their buying journey, how likely they will go on the whole journey with the seller, and how significant the opportunity might be both in developing the seller's strategy and tactics for winning the deal. The Transformational Seller will prioritise resources and make better go/no-go decisions on each opportunity.
- Tier 1 Qualification is based on the BANT structure (**budget, authority, need, timescales**) and is useful for assessing the quality and potential of an opportunity.
- Tier 2 Qualification is based on the CASE structure (**characteristics, alternatives, scope, emotional drivers**) and enables the seller to develop their 'case' or win plan.
- Creating a formal structure and discipline for the seller's qualification is one of the most simple and

effective ways of substantially improving sales performance and pipeline management.

- Qualification is an ongoing process and not a tick box exercise. It relies on the Transformational Seller delving deeper and developing both the breadth and quality of intelligence around the opportunity.
- Advancements in CRM tools and the use of AI will support the Transformational Seller in making better decisions around sales opportunities, but this will require increasing discipline from the seller to ask the right questions and engage with a broader range of stakeholders.

CHAPTER 9
QUESTIONING FOR INFLUENCE

I keep six honest serving men.

(They taught me all I knew);

Their names are What and Why and When

And How and Where and Who.

The Elephant's Child, Rudyard Kipling

The art of great rhetoric, the ability to influence through powerful speech, emerged around 600 BC with the pre-Socratic Sophists. They were trained to use oratorical persuasion in legal disputes.

Even today, barristers are amongst the best practitioners of rhetoric. Interestingly, they are also some of the best questioners, trained to extract crucial information, even confessions, from witnesses on the stand. Think of Tom Cruise interrogating Jack Nicholson in *A Few Good Men*, culminating in the infamous line that exposed the latter's guilt: "You can't handle the truth!"

Whilst great speeches can inspire people to act, there's more to influence and persuasion than simply articulating your point of view. Dale Carnegie highlighted this almost a century ago and since then it has been frequently recognised that questioning holds the key to influence. More specifically, asking the right questions enables sellers to navigate their way through their client's business, develop a greater understanding of their goals, glean how they are performing and what is getting in the way of their achievement.

Questioning is the most powerful implement in a seller's tool-kit, helping them to establish and build great working relationships. It helps them also to control and direct the conversation, explore the gap between the customer's success criteria and challenges and create a compelling case for change.

Despite this, many sales executives struggle to ask questions, or more accurately, they struggle to ask the *right* questions, or else they stop asking questions far too early in the process. We have mulled this over for many years as to why and our best guess is that for many sellers, talking is just easier than listening.

There's also perhaps a fear that encouraging the customer to do the talking relinquishes control of the conversation, when in fact the opposite is true. The person asking the questions is the one who is firmly in control of both the direction and the outcome of the conversation. It's a concept we refer to as the 'Control Paradox'.

How many times have you found yourself drifting off when someone was talking to you? It's something that happens a lot. Questions have the opposite effect.

What colour is your front door?

There's a good chance that the image which came to your mind from the question was that of your front door. This illustrates the power of questions. They do much more than gather information; they enable us to focus and direct people's thoughts.

Questioning is a highly developed skill. You don't always get the answers you are expecting and need to react and respond to keep the conversation moving. This is perhaps another reason why people prefer to pitch than to ask. Pitching what you already know about is easier and more 'Comfort Zone' oriented than allowing a conversation to go in an 'unknown' direction.

The Control Paradox

This is an example of what we have observed.

Seller: How often do you have a problem with getting the machines back up and running?

Customer: It tends to be more of an issue with our remote sites where it can take longer for them to get an engineer out.

Seller: Typically, how long could that be?

Customer: It might be a day or two before the problem gets resolved.

Seller: That must be frustrating. One of our key benefits is that we can have an engineer on site within four hours regardless of location. We have significantly more engineers than any of our competitors and have fifteen depots up and down the country that are manned 24/7 so we can dispatch help whenever it's needed. All are fully trained and certified and carry spares with them so they can fix most problems on site.

Customer: That sounds great. Is that four-hour timeframe guaranteed?

Seller: Well, we can't actually guarantee it, we are dependent on factors such a traffic, and whether there are other emergencies we are dealing with. We do have an SLA with customers that we will get to them within the four-hour timeframe.

Customer: What compensation do you give for not hitting the SLA?

Seller: That's usually something we agree with you as part of the overall package.

Customer: How often do you meet that SLA with your customers?

Seller: I don't have that exact figure to hand but it's very rare that we don't hit our SLAs. Let me get back to you on that one.

Notice how quickly this conversation gets out of control for the seller. Initially their questions elicited a particular challenge for the customer, at which point the seller felt the compulsion to pitch back the solution. As soon as they do, the customer becomes the one asking questions about guarantees and compensation, which is not what the seller wanted to be discussing at this stage.

To regain control of the conversation they need to start asking questions again. One of the best sales individual's we've ever worked with was renowned in such circumstances for responding with: "That's a great question, what makes you ask?" Answering a question with a question enables you to buy some thinking time and regain control of the conversation.

THE POWER OF QUESTIONING – PRESENT, PAST, FUTURE AND CHANGE QUESTIONS

When we meet with sales directors or chief revenue officers (CRO), we need to establish how they are targeted and what those specific targets are. Typically, they will have a revenue and perhaps also a margin target to match. These targets almost invariably increase year on year, creating a lot of pressure.

As part of the SCOPE Model for discovery meetings we would focus initially on these targets and define the customer's success criteria using **present**, **past**, **future** and **change** type questions such as:

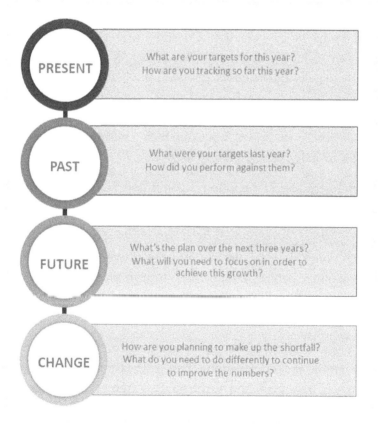

PRESENT

What are your targets for this year?
How are you tracking so far this year?

PAST

What were your targets last year?
How did you perform against them?

FUTURE

What's the plan over the next three years?
What will you need to focus on in order to achieve this growth?

CHANGE

How are you planning to make up the shortfall?
What do you need to do differently to continue to improve the numbers?

Figure 9.1: Present, Past, Future and Change Questions

This structure encourages the customer not only to articulate their current objectives but also to reflect on how these have changed and are likely to change in the future. The idea is simple, if selling is all about 'change' then focusing the customer on how their desired or required outcomes are changing is a good place to start.

Whether the customer is behind or even ahead of the curve this year, they either need to change what they are doing now or be prepared to change and enhance what they are doing moving forward to continue to hit those ever-increasing targets.

The other aspect to consider is how to use differing timeframes to open up the conversation. Questioning starts in the present: this year's target; current performance. We do this because people usually find it easier to open up when talking about the present. Notice how when you meet people for the first time you are most likely to ask about what they currently do for a living, where they live, how old their children are. In other words, focusing on the present tense.

As you get to build a relationship and develop greater rapport, so your questions may venture into the past: Where did you study? Where did you work before? Where did you grow up?

Finally, once you get deeper into the conversation, you may start asking people about their future plans (beyond this weekend or their holidays), although invariably, conversation rarely gets this deep on a first encounter in a social setting.

The present, past, future and change structure is a neat way of broadening the conversation and embedding the idea that change is inevitable and a constant. It frames the customer's thinking around the need to respond to these changes accordingly.

Whilst we have used the example of a sales director, whose objectives are typically ruled by strict performance metrics, every decision maker will have quantifiable objectives to meet.

It may be that your customer is in production and will be tasked with output, efficiencies, production quotas or cost reductions. A HR professional may be targeted on employee engagement, absenteeism, staff retention and recruitment. An IT director could be responsible for uptime, security or helpdesk resolution statistics.

Whatever discipline your customer is in, they will have objectives (both business and personal) that they need to achieve and the present, past, future and change questions become the launch-pad for such conversations.

NO PAIN, NO GAIN

Previous chapters explored the idea that a customer's drive for change will come through the recognition of a **compelling event** or the **erosion of satisfaction**. These become more acutely highlighted through the use of the SCOPE Model for discovery and the exploration of the gap between their defined **success outcomes** and the **challenges** they are likely to face.

We often refer to these as the customer 'pain points': those things that aren't working as well as they should, the factors that are making the achievement of goals more difficult or preventing the customer from taking advantage of potential opportunities.

Discussing pains isn't comfortable, particularly for the customer, but that's the reason why you should do it. If you want to demonstrate how you can help customers realise their objectives, you must be prepared to have frank and honest discussions about the factors that could prevent them from doing so.

Exploring pains means highlighting and exposing the weaknesses within your customer's current arrangements, much like a dentist checking your teeth and finding that one of them needs a filling. Whilst a good dentist won't inflict any more pain than is necessary, they may need to probe further to understand the severity of the issue. What they will do is explain what could happen if you fail to get it fixed.

Many sellers fail by jumping too quickly into 'solution mode'. On identifying a customer's pain, they move immediately to present the solution without further exploration or additional probing to fully explore the issue and its potential impact moving forward.

The customer may baulk at fixing the problem because of:

- **Inertia** – the pain is not considered severe enough to warrant any action (there are plenty of imperfections in all facets of our lives that we are prepared to live with).
- **Finance** – they don't want to spend money to put the problem right.
- **Lack of awareness** – they haven't recognised all the potential ramifications of the pain if they ignore it.
- **Time and stress** – there is a lot of perceived time and hassle involved in putting the problem right.

These four factors link back to the fear of change (or apathy), and the importance of the seller helping the customer to appreciate that the risk of *not changing* or acting is far greater than making the change. Rhetoric can play its part, but in isolation, rhetoric can sound like more 'feature bashing' or worse still 'fear mongering'.

The Transformational Seller understands the importance of metaphorically 'pressing on the tooth' so that the customer feels the pain far more acutely and therefore also appreciates the value of the solution.

THE CATALYST FOR CHANGE

The world as we have created it is a process of our thinking. It cannot be changed without changing our thinking.

Albert Einstein

Transformational Sellers are **catalysts for change**. They don't tell their customers to change, they use insightful questioning related to the customer's own desired outcomes to enable them to see for themselves and, more importantly, express in their own words the compelling need for change.

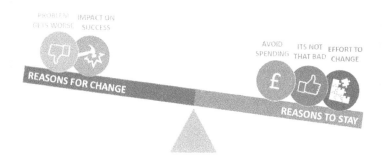

Figure 9.2: The Balance of Change

The challenge for customers is that there are always reasons not to change. These reasons are often emotional rather than logical and they can outweigh the reasons for change. Therefore, our case for change has to be much more significant and needs to have greater mass and impact on tipping the balance in favour of action.

Questioning to create the need for change – an example

Steve: We were conducting a pipeline review for a seller on an opportunity that they had been working on for months. Their main contact was the production manager in a manufacturing plant and this contact had been working on a proposal to completely upgrade a well-worn production line.

Over that time, the various components had been repaired and replaced. Recently these requirements had become greater, like an old car that spends more time in the garage than on the road.

Whilst each individual repair or replacement might range from a few hundred to a few thousand pounds each, the cost of a complete upgrade was going to be hundreds of thousands of pounds.

The seller was frustrated that the sales process had stalled; he'd forecast that this deal should have already landed. However, because the expenditure went well beyond the customer's repair budget, it needed to go through a formal process and gain approval at board level. Initially, the seller wasn't unduly worried as the case for a complete overhaul was fairly cut and dried. However, as time dragged on, he became increasingly concerned that the project would get shelved.

The seller said to us: "The customer knows they need it and I know that a company of their size should be able to raise the capital – I can't understand why they are procrastinating."

We've seen this scenario played out in numerous interactions with sellers; we've lost count of the number of 'no-brainer' sales opportunities that stall. It didn't take long to get to the bottom of why this deal wasn't going anywhere.

We started with the customer's **initial interest** (their **compelling event** or **erosion of satisfaction**). The conversation went like this:

Us: "So what are your customer's objectives? What targets or KPIs are they measured on?"

Seller: "The usual ones you would expect; uptime [the percentage of time the production line is up and running] and cost reduction. They've also been tasked with reducing energy consumption from both a cost and environmental credentials perspective. Our upgrade would actually reduce the energy consumption considerably, which is why it's so puzzling that they are stalling."

Us: "great, now let's get down to the details. What level of uptime they are targeted at? How are they performing against this? What are their energy consumption targets?"

The seller established that these were the objectives but not the actual figures of what they had to achieve, how they were performing and why (i.e., the gap between **success** and **challenges**).

Whilst on a conceptual level the idea of implementing a major upgrade made sense, without probing and quantifying the core of the problems for the customer, the **erosion of satisfaction** failed to be compelling enough for the customer to act with any degree of urgency.

The balance for the 'reasons to change' versus the 'reasons to stay the same' was weighted in favour of staying the same. The change would require a huge investment, it will require downtime and a loss of production. It also requires customer effort to go through the budget process and a degree of risk (the risk of the results not delivering the required outcomes) and the potential damage to the firm's own reputation.

Whilst the customer was on their buying journey, they were not committed to seeing it all the way through; change was viewed as optional and not a necessity.

QUESTIONING APPROACH – FROM OUTSIDE TO INSIDE

We have seen how the use of present, past, future and change questions provide a structure at the early stages of the sales process by creating the need for change. These need to be explored at deeper levels, because:

- It can be costly to assume that a customer willing to talk about change is committed to seeing it all the way through.
- It's important to recognise that even where the customer is fully committed to completing their buying journey, they will almost certainly need others within their organisation to go on the same journey with them.

- The customer may be fully committed to making the change, but you still need to convince them why that change should be undertaken with you.

Customers don't always respond well to being told that they have an issue. They don't necessarily like being told that:

- Their current suppliers are falling short of giving them what they really need (especially if they were involved in the selection of those suppliers).
- Their business is prone to risk (which implies that they should have already recognised this).
- As things stand, they are unlikely to achieve their goals (now *they* can't handle the truth!).

The customer needs to identify these things for themselves and, just as importantly, to verbalise them. Our questions, therefore, need to take the customer on a journey that reinforces the need for change and steers them towards the recognition of the issues and pains that the offering can solve.

The Transformational Seller needs to use the questioning process to probe deeper into the core of the customer's potential issues and pains. Like when peeling an onion, the seller should work from the outside to the core.

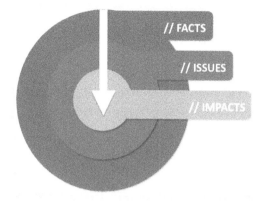

Figure 9.3: Questioning at Three Levels: From Outside to Inside

Through questioning from **outside to inside**, the Transformational Seller takes the customer on a journey from the surface where things are immediately visible, into the core. At the core sit the customer's key drivers and emotions that will ultimately lead to change. The seller needs to structure their questions in the following way:

- **Information and facts** – the who, what, when, where, why and how. In addition to the customer's key outcomes, objectives and targets, the seller should look at what they currently have in place, how they manage the tasks in hand, and where they currently source their materials from.
- **Issues and challenges** – the seller should invite the customer to discuss how well these current arrangements work and the typical results that they have seen. The seller then needs to get them to outline the things that need to change and any issues that might arise as a result. The seller must probe further to understand why the results are what they are currently and the potential risks to achieving their objectives, i.e., what could get in the way.

- **Impact on outcomes** – next the seller can take this a stage further and examine the potential impact that these issues and challenges are having on the customer achieving their desired success outcomes and what it means for them and the business. (Critically, this includes the impact on their customers.)

Having observed thousands of sales calls across many different industries, we have seen the enormous power of when sellers have taken this approach, reinforcing the **compelling event** or **erosion of satisfaction** that drives the customer to change, establishing and reprioritising their wish list accordingly.

Our key observations:

- Despite the potentially powerful impact that the questioning approach can have, sellers have a tendency to fall short. They are more comfortable asking questions that establish the information and facts but find it difficult to get into deeper areas.
- The customer verbalising the impact of issues on their chances of success is critical to their commitment in wanting to resolve them.
- The customer truly believing in the need for change is fundamental to ensuring they gain consensus from the other stakeholders within the DMU.
- Without exploring the impact that these issues have on the success criteria, the seller doesn't truly understand the strength of the case for change, leading to weaker negotiation, and a failure to handle customer objections or to create any sense of urgency to make a decision.

Delegates have described this questioning process as being something akin to therapy for their customers.

How many psychotherapists does it take to change a lightbulb?
Only one, but the lightbulb really has to want to change!

Questioning from the outside in: an example

Earlier we looked at the example of the seller feeling frustrated at the stalling of a large 'no-brainer' sale. We established that without having fully explored the customer's success criteria and required outcomes (using present, past, future and change questions) then the seller cannot be sure how much commitment to change they have created.

Furthermore, we were keen to look at how else the seller could have continued the conversation and strengthened the case for their solution.

Us: "Ok. What about the impact of the repairs and replacements on uptime. How much time has been lost due breakdowns and unscheduled repairs?"

Seller: "Quite a lot."

Us: "What figure can the customer put on the amount of downtime they actually incurred?"

Seller: "I didn't ask."

Us: "Ok. What's the cost per hour of downtime for this production line? In other words, how much money are they losing every time they have to halt production?"

Seller: "Thousands I'd imagine, I didn't discuss an exact figure."

You can see the pattern. Without a detailed level of questioning that builds not only the facts but also the issues and their impact on outcomes, we have only limited reinforcement of the case for our proposal and one that is unlikely to overcome the potential barriers that will prevent it from going ahead.

These questions are fundamental as they *quantify the pain*. Remember the dentist from earlier in the chapter? "How much does it hurt when I do this?" The seller's questions need to help the customer establish their own level of pain. In some cases, this will be easier to measure; establishing the cost of aborted transactions on the customer's website or the cost of absenteeism on the business may be well defined. Other issues may be harder to quantify.

Either way, the Transformational Seller asks these questions even where they suspect the customer can't give a precise answer. In fact, the customer *not* being able to answer can wield more power than the customer having an answer. Knowing that something could be very costly, but having no idea exactly how much, can deliver greater discomfort than when they have it all scoped out. How do you quantify, for example, the cost of a badly damaged reputation following a major data breach?

Level 1 – Information and Facts	Utilise: who, what, when, where, why, how. In terms of success criteria, current performance, current approaches, suppliers, resources.
Level 2 – Issues and Challenges	Invite the customer to discuss the following with the current/proposed approach to achieving their objectives: • difficulties • issues • challenges • problems • barriers • risks • concerns
Level 3 – Impact on Outcomes	Explore the following with the customer: • impact • effect • implications • consequences • ramifications • repercussions • costs (financially and in terms of business)

Table 9.1: Three Level Questioning from Outside to Inside

BUILDING VALUE FROM OUTSIDE TO INSIDE

We have observed how the use of this questioning approach could help create a stronger case for the customer to act. Similarly, you can use it to build a compelling case for your own differentiators.

Reflecting back to the customer buying journey in Chapter 3, we reviewed how the Transformational Seller needs to influence the customer's wish list to ensure that their own product or service's key differentiators were elevated on it.

This approach of questioning from outside to inside can be used specifically within the context of a core differentiator or selling point which may form part of your overall offering.

For example, if having a 'premium service' for faster delivery is part of your offering, you need to ask what the potential issues associated with slow or late deliveries are and, even more importantly, how that would affect their customers. Most businesses have major 'supply-chain reactions' which can have serious knock-on effects when functioning poorly.

For example, in the construction industry, not getting an early delivery on site might mean sub-contractors standing idle or having to be removed, potentially having to be paid, or if not, the issues associated with them moving to another job making it difficult to get them back on-site when required. This could result in increased costs, projects over-running potentially incurring heavy penalty clauses and damaging the customer's reputation with the client, resulting in a permanent loss of business, and creating a 'lose-lose' situation for everyone.

It's these further areas of exploration that the Transformational Seller recognises: it's not enough to just build a compelling reason for change; you need to create a powerful case as to why *you* should be their partner of choice, through your offering, insights and value proposition.

FOCUSING ON THE FUTURE

One of the fundamental differences between the Consultative Seller and the Transformational Seller is the latter's ability to solve not only the *known* but also the *unknown problems*. This includes being able to assist the customer in planning ahead and providing solutions that not only solve their immediate issues, but also mitigate the known and unknown risks ahead.

As we have seen recently, despite most businesses having claimed to embrace technology, how few of these were genuinely geared up for the remote working situation they were confronted with lockdowns in 2020?

Businesses often react when it is either too late, extremely costly or when it is only absolutely necessary. The Transformational Seller questions the different realistic 'worst case' scenarios with a view to prevention rather than cure.

What we realised during the pandemic was that unforeseen situations can arise extremely quickly and have a massive impact on businesses and lives. Whilst we could not prevent Covid-19 from happening, being ready at the outset to face such a situation would have helped more companies to survive. There will be other 'mission critical' situations over the next decade and beyond: the potential of further pandemics; wars; terrorist atrocities; cyber-attacks; and the ever-growing global environmental problems. Businesses will need to consider these and plan accordingly.

The 'open versus closed' question debate

Historically, there has been a lot of debate on the importance of open and closed questions within the sales process. Conventional thinking states that an open question elicits an 'open' answer and a closed question merely a 'yes' or a 'no' response.

In reality, it doesn't always work that way. Ask an open question such as: "How was your weekend?" and you may just get "fine!" Alternatively, ask a closed question such as: "Did you have a good weekend?" you might get a detailed account of the last 48 hours.

People will provide an open or closed answer based on how they feel, rather than necessarily how the question was worded. However, there is a far more subtle and more powerful distinction between the two that becomes important when you are encouraging your customer to explore the unknowns – particularly as you work your way towards the 'inside'.

Imagine you ask the following as a closed question:

"Do you have any issues with...?"

The subtext of this question suggests possibility, that the customer may or may not have experienced issues. In the absence of something springing to mind, it's often easier for the customer to respond with a "no". It's the same as when you ask: "Have you seen my car keys?"

We will now 'open' this question up:

"What issues have you had with...?"

There is an inherent assumption within this question that the customer has experienced issues. The customer will also accept this assumption unconsciously and is more likely to reflect before answering.

So, when utilising the questioning structures during this chapter, consider how and when you are using open versus closed questions to ensure you are provoking the right level of thinking and response.

At home you could also try: "Where did you last see my car keys?"

Exercise: Questioning

Think of a typical issue you have helped other clients to solve in your industry that a prospect or existing client of yours has not yet identified.

Next, start to formulate a set of questions using the outside to inside approach – from the factual to issues to impact, with the aim of getting the customer to expand on their thinking.

CHAPTER SUMMARY

- Questioning is the most important tool for the Transformational Seller. It is the basis on which they form effective business relationships, control the direction of the conversation, establish the customer's needs and create a compelling reason for change.
- Despite the importance of questioning being well established it remains a major gap for many sellers.
- The use of **present**, **past**, **future** and **change** questions can be useful in opening the customer up to recognising the need for change and helping them along the early stages of their buying journey.
- Understanding and exploring the customer's pains helps them to continue on their buying journey and creates a greater degree of urgency for them to act. The seller becomes the **catalyst for change** in helping the customer to recognise the potential consequences and pitfalls of inaction.
- Questioning from **outside to inside** goes from visible information and facts, to exploring the issues and challenges and reviewing the impact, or potential impact, on the customer's stated outcomes. This approach can be used not only to reinforce the need for a different solution, but also the need for a specific aspect of the seller's offering (ideally one that differentiates the seller from the competition).
- One of the major differences that the Transformational Seller demonstrates over their consultative peers is the ability to not only solve the customer's known problems but, more importantly, identify and solve the problems that the customer hasn't recognised. They do

this through effective questioning combined with their ability to leverage expertise, which is explored in the next chapter.

CHAPTER 10
LEVERAGING EXPERTISE

Life isn't about being an expert in everything.

It's about being an expert on one thing and offering it to the world.

Bo Sanchez

As a Transformational Seller, your expertise enables you to guide the customer through their buying journey, to help them to identify the problems that they were potentially unaware of; opening their eyes to what is possible; guiding them on the criteria they should be using to make their decisions, inspiring them to make changes; and collaborating with your customer to create the business case that will enable them to achieve their desired outcomes.

Your expertise comes from numerous sources, not least from within your own organisation where vast experience and know-how have enabled the organisation to create and market its products and services. Within your organisation sits the tacit knowledge of thousands of sales calls, client interactions, problems solved, and results achieved that provide the basis for future client interactions. It's worth remembering that the Transformational Seller, in their pursuit of becoming their customer's trusted expert, does not necessarily have all the answers themselves but is the conduit to them.

In the most critical aspects of our day-to-day lives, we generally seek out experts; we get an accountant or IFA to manage our finances; we hire a lawyer to deal with our legal issues; and we employ a mechanic to service our car. So, when customers are looking to improve their operations, drive greater sales, reduce their carbon footprint, elevate their brand or protect their assets, they also need to look to experts for guidance.

SOURCES OF KNOWLEDGE AND EXPERTISE

Expertise is more than having a lot of knowledge, although that is a starting point. Turning your knowledge into expertise is the principle of applying knowledge to different situations to provide customers with greater understanding and direction to achieve better results. Your knowledge comes from three broad sources: product or service, industry experience and customer-specific understanding.

Product/Service Knowledge

This is usually the starting point for businesses when on-boarding new sales people. A lot of time and effort is spent making sure that they understand the main features and key selling points of their products and services.

Traditionally, product knowledge has been viewed as the most important component a seller needs to be effective. For those who can recall their sales induction programmes from the past, they were often focused on product knowledge.

Our work with private equity companies has introduced us to numerous start-up businesses looking to drive sales growth. We've observed how many entrepreneurs and founders take on the role of the main seller (and sometimes how hard they find it to let go). They argue that as the product was their brainchild, no one else is able to promote it with the same degree of knowledge and passion.

However, it's this passion and intimate knowledge of their products that often leads to evangelising, and evangelising is the basis for a Transactional Approach.

Over-emphasis on product knowledge *at the expense* of enabling sellers to enhance their broader knowledge base can be a disabler for selling. It creates a product-focused and, therefore, more transactional mentality.

Whilst product knowledge is important, on its own it is not expertise.

INDUSTRY EXPERIENCE

When we refer to 'industry' we mean both the vertical and horizontal aspects of your offering. It may be that you work exclusively within one vertical sector (e.g., products and services into the construction industry) or with a particular horizontal sector (e.g., HR software used by HR professionals in any business) or that you specialise in a specific horizontal and vertical sector (e.g., HR software specifically for the construction industry).

However, you define your market, your industry knowledge is gained through being immersed in what you do on a daily basis. This becomes a key focus for the Transformational Seller who:

- Regularly reviews the PESTLE (political, economic, social, technological, legislative and environmental) factors for their own industry. It's these factors that are likely to be the greatest source of change for the customer. They drive **compelling events** or an **erosion of satisfaction** and are key to engagement with customers.
- Analyses and reviews the information they have gleaned from their existing customers: what they are doing, what's working well, and which particular challenges are impacting them in terms of achieving their goals and objectives.
- Researches the competition, both in terms of how they are developing their offering and also by gaining feedback from customers in terms of the strengths and weaknesses of their own offering, which supports them in targeting questions to build value in their key differentiators.

CUSTOMER UNDERSTANDING

As we have discussed in previous chapters, your ability to differentiate yourself and your offering is not always based on your product or service capability.

The Transformational Seller's most powerful differentiator is themselves. This is evidenced through their being extremely curious in relation to their customers, and their ability to question effectively and listen accordingly.

The Transformation Seller is not just concerned with what their customers do, they want to know how they do it and, most importantly, why. They ask: how long have they been doing it that way, what prompted them to change, and what other options they have tried?

There is often a marked reluctance amongst sellers to ask too many questions, or else they tend to follow the script that they are given without thinking or responding to the answers the customer provides: questioning on autopilot, and not actively listening to each response given.

Customer understanding or questioning on autopilot

Steve: We once worked with a business focusing on supporting their customers with lead and revenue generation. We observed numerous sales meetings where, as part of the discovery, sellers questioned the customer about their turnover before moving on to other aspects of the business. Establishing turnover was a requirement of their company's qualification criteria.

We asked: "So what does that information give you and what do you do with it?"

The general consensus was that it enabled them to gauge the size of the company they were dealing with.

We then asked: "How does that help you from a sales perspective?" The group weren't sure; it was just something they had been trained to ask.

The reality is that information could be valuable but only if the conversation had been broadened to understand the following:

- Current revenue targets and outcomes.
- ·How that revenue had changed over the recent years (grown, flat-lined or declined).
- The reasons behind that change (market growth, market saturation, new product development, competitor activity, economic factors).
- Revenue predictions and targets over the next year, three years and five years and why these are important to the company's strategy.

Now they had information that was relevant and useful to the sales conversation.

OVERCOMING THE 'WHY' PROBLEM

In exploring the customer in more detail, understanding 'why' uncovers their drivers, motives, thinking and assumptions. However, asking the direct question 'why' can come with negative connotations, with the recipient seeing it as a challenge or criticism to their approach or past decisions.

The question "why did you choose your current supplier?" could elicit a defensive response, which is unlikely to aid collaboration and a commitment to change.

By replacing the 'why' with a 'what' or a 'how', this can be a far more productive way of opening your customer up to a better response. This means that "why did you choose your current supplier?" now becomes "what were the key factors that influenced your choice of supplier?" or "how did you go about selecting them as a supplier?"

TURNING YOUR KNOWLEDGE INTO EXPERTISE

Knowledge is knowing that the tomato is a fruit.

Wisdom is not putting it in a fruit salad!

Anon

Armed with an ever-increasing repertoire of knowledge, the Transformational Seller needs to consider two aspects:

- How to turn their knowledge into expertise.
- How to deliver this expertise in a way that delivers impact and creates a 'moment' for the customer.

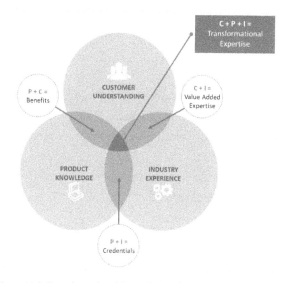

Figure 10.1: Transformational Expertise Model

The knowledge gained through these three different sources becomes valuable when it is combined to create expertise that can elevate your status as a Transformational Seller and move the sales opportunity forward. If we look at the various combinations we see:

Product Knowledge + Industry Experience = Credentials

We refer to this expertise as **credentials**. Included within this might be case studies and references from other clients which will typically include the problems they were facing, what you did to overcome them and the successful outcome(s) they experienced.

Whilst credentials have an important role, their effectiveness is reliant on making them relevant and impactful to your prospect. They are often introduced in the early stages to advertise your offering but fail to fully resonate because the customer:

- Doesn't recognise the problem that you solved in relation to their own business.
- Is focused on a different outcome to the one illustrated in the case study.
- Views their business as being very different from the customer in the case study.

We see this in 'story-telling', which could and should be a very powerful sales tool. Yet often these stories lack real bite, because the seller is unable to establish the relevance of the story back to the customer and their specific situation.

The power of successful story-telling, just like any good film, play or book, is where you feel an emotional connection to the characters, their predicament and outcome. The customer needs to feel a similar connection to the issues and challenges faced in the case study, and how these were resolved.

Product Knowledge + Customer Understanding = Benefits

When we talk about **benefits**, it's this combination of product and customer knowledge that we are referring to. Benefits are important aspects of your product or service and how they relate to the customer and the specific problems that they are looking to solve and the outcomes they are looking to achieve.

'Benefits Selling' has been the cornerstone of sales practice for around sixty years, since the phrase was coined in the 1960s as part of the psychology behind the sales revolution. Whilst a lot has happened since then, the concept is still an important aspect of both the Transactional and, more specifically, the Consultative approach to selling.

Whilst benefits are still critical in developing a compelling sales argument, the combination of product and customer knowledge without industry knowledge tends towards a focus on solving only the known issues – those that the customer has identified for themselves, and therefore, frequently the customer identifies the solution for themselves too. As such, differentiation becomes difficult to establish as this becomes little more than an advanced form of order taking.

> Customer Understanding + Industry Experience = Value Add Expertise

The combining of customer understanding and industry experience is what we refer to as **value added expertise**. It helps to develop the seller's relationship, status and credibility with the customer and is very effective in creating those 'oh s**t' moments. However, unless you can link it back to your offering it may have only limited value in the long run.

There needs to be a word of caution extended to your value-added expertise to avoid inadvertently acting as a free consultancy service for your customer.

The concept of the trusted adviser has long been advocated in sales and in more recent times, The Challenger Approach, and its emphasis on teaching the customer has amplified this view. Companies fight over the idea of being regarded as 'thought leaders' and market themselves accordingly, and professional networks such as LinkedIn are not short of individuals willing to offer their insights and observations.

The important point here is that at some stage you need to be able to make a direct link back to your products and services. We have heard stories of sellers giving up hours of their time operating as trusted advisers, helping customers to write specifications, review designs or help conduct audits which utilised their skills and wider industry knowledge only to gain nothing in return.

The assumption made is that such activity drives greater customer loyalty and therefore increases the chance of the sale or repeat orders. In the New World, customer loyalty will be harder to maintain, with decisions increasingly made by committees and disparate groups of stakeholders. The fact that you previously helped out one of these stakeholders may not carry as much weight as you might hope.

This doesn't mean that you shouldn't help clients out or find ways to add value. It just means that you should be wary of falling into the trap of the 'passive seller', whose main strategy is to offer excellent customer service instead of actual selling.

> Customer Understanding + Industry Experience + Product Knowledge
> = Transformational Expertise

The sweet spot for the Transformational Seller is where they combine their experience of the industry, their customer understanding, and knowledge of their products and services to create and deliver their expertise. When they combine all three elements it enables them to:

- Highlight a problem that the customer didn't know that they had.
- Understand the upstream and downstream effects associated with both the problem and the potential solutions.
- Focus on the outcomes their customer is looking to achieve.
- Demonstrate how other customers have overcome their problems and the role the seller played in expediting this.
- Elevate the importance of certain aspects of the seller' functionality or service, in areas not highlighted by the competition (not necessarily because they couldn't offer it but because they didn't appreciate the significance of it).

Transformational Selling – an example

Bryn: We once engaged with a customer whose sales team needed help in driving higher profit margins. They were a premium brand and well respected for quality and reliability. However, their market was in downturn, fewer customers were buying and those that were, were easily tempted by cheaper offerings. As a result, the sales team were constantly faced with price objections and often capitulated on these. Whilst the company was still generating decent revenue, the average profit was extremely low, and on certain deals they were making almost nothing.

Having seen many examples of their sellers capitulating at the negotiation stage of the sale, the client wanted to focus on improving the negotiation skills of their team. We spent time exploring what was happening, interviewing and observing the sales and management teams to get a clearer idea of what was going wrong.

Had we been operating purely as Consultative Sellers we would have put together a development programme based around improving their skills and confidence around handling price objections and negotiations.

However, with a strong understanding of sales methodology and the customer's sales process, we needed to inject into the discussion and recommendations our industry experience. Having previously worked with numerous sales teams across multiple verticals we knew that problems with price objections and negotiations were usually symptomatic of problems further upstream (i.e., earlier in the sales process).

We used our industry experience to focus further investigation on the initial stages of the sales process, how the team went about conducting their discovery meetings, how they utilised and leveraged differentiators, and their investigation and questioning of customer pain points. It was clear that their problems stemmed from a lack of building value in their proposition in the first place. Questioning, in many cases, was limited to information gathering and, therefore, they were failing to create a compelling need for the client to invest in a premium option.

We recommended a programme with a heavier focus on discovery rather than pure negotiation, together with developing their front-line management population to equip them with the skills to observe and coach their sales teams in the field.

By implementing this approach, the sales team achieved a fifty-two percent increase in their average gross profit over the course of the next year, which their managers reinforced. Interestingly, we ended up not even touching negotiation skills until after this had been achieved!

The lesson here is that the Transformational Seller has to go beyond just making product recommendations to match the customer's immediate problems.

Coincidentally, the approach that we took with the client was not dissimilar to the approach we taught their sales team to adopt in terms of leveraging broader industry experience within the sales process.

LEVERAGING EXPERTISE - THE APPROACH

I'm playing all the right notes;

but not necessarily in the right order.

Eric Morecambe

Since the launch of *The Challenger Sale*, many sales and marketing organisations have worked on supporting their sales teams with the concept of creating **insights**. We've spoken to many organisations who have tried to adopt this approach as a mechanism of equipping sellers with the ability to wow, educate or shock their customers into action.

The general premise is that businesses supply a number of key insights to their sales teams, using customer and industry research. The sales team then tend to sprinkle them like confetti into sales meetings and presentations. The end result has been the rise of the 'did you know that…' sales phenomenon, placing all the emphasis on the 'what to say' but not 'how to say it'.

Expertise is not simply a case of throwing a fact or statistic into the conversation. Leveraging your expertise is the process of expanding your customer's thinking by examining the assumptions that they are making, enabling them to see different perspectives and providing new or different frames of reference. The question for many is, how to do this.

If you want to leverage your expertise to support your sales conversation, the approach to take follows these three key steps, as in Figure 10.2.

Figure 10.2: The Three Steps to Leverage Experience

Set-Up to establish relevance. This means introducing an idea or topic and, through questioning, encouraging the customer to share their thoughts and observations around it, referring back to previous information that the customer has shared with you.

Deliver by providing expertise. Having opened up the conversation, you can then provide them with your expertise on the topic, the observations you have made and the conclusions that you and your organisation have reached.

Explore the potential fall-out from this for the customer. You can now allow the customer to elaborate on their thinking as a result of the information and expertise you have provided.

Let's look at how this approach might work for the example we gave earlier. In this case, our expertise told us that poor negotiation was often down to insufficient discovery and value building at earlier stages in the process.

Using the 'did you know' approach

Customer issue	We need to improve our margins and gross profit.
	Our sales team capitulate on price and are too keen to discount to try to win the deal. Therefore, we need you to develop their negotiation skills to drive margin up.
Our analysis	In our experience, it's probably not your negotiation skills that's the problem. Through our experience of working with hundreds of other clients, the number one root cause of issues regarding price and negotiation is in fact a lack of effective discovery and a failure to build value in differentiators.

Here we can see the 'did you know' approach merely told the customer that their assumptions were probably incorrect and therefore their proposed solution was misguided. In effect, we have told the customer that they are wrong.

How often have you ever won an argument by telling someone that they are wrong?

Using the SDE leverage expertise approach

	We need to improve our margins and gross profit.
Customer	
	Our sales team capitulate on price and are too keen to discount to try and win the deal. Therefore, we need you to develop their negotiation skills to drive the margins up.

Our analysis	Why do you think this is happening at the negotiation stage?
SET UP	Why do you think their confidence is low?
	What are the sales teams doing to build value and differentiate during the early stages of the process?
DELIVER	In working across hundreds of clients, we've found that the number one root cause of issues regarding price and negotiation is in fact a lack of effective discovery and a failure to differentiate.
	What monitoring and observation have you done around the discovery stage of the sales process?
EXPLORE	What observations do you have around the sales teams' ability to monetise the problem they are solving for their customer?
	How could the sales team be better leveraging your differentiators?

When we review the leveraging expertise approach, we can see that:

- We use questions during the **set-up** phase to encourage the customer to talk about the observations which led to their initial conclusions, before questioning them on their thoughts as to what was happening in the Discovery Phase.

- The customer is already starting to think about potential inadequacies within that phase of the sales process at the point where we then **deliver** our message which now resonates with them.
- Having delivered the message, the questions then encourage the customer to reflect on this and **explore** what needs to change as a result.

Notice, here, the approach to asking questions in both the **set-up** and **explore** phases. It's these questions that start to challenge the assumptions that the customer is making and allow them to reach different conclusions for themselves.

We are also leveraging all three aspects of Transformational Expertise: Customer Understanding, Product Knowledge and Industry Experience to demonstrate our expertise.

We can look at an example in a different industry.

The SDE leverage expertise approach

Here we want to share our knowledge and expertise around the uncertainty and risk of a security breach.

SET UP	What approach do you take to security and protection?
	How often do you review your approach?
	What experience have you had regarding attacks and breaches?

DELIVER	According to a recent Gartner Report, sixty-four percent of breaches go undetected. Those that are detected take on average seven months to come to light.
EXPLORE	With that in mind, what is your biggest concern regarding security?
	Where do you feel that you are most vulnerable?
	What plans do you have to review your security system?

Note the final questions that we asked in each of these examples. By using open questions, the inherent assumptions become quite powerful. The customer's thinking is directed towards the 'better leveraging of differentiators' or 'reviewing the system' as a *fait accompli*. The fact that they are (or at least should be) reviewing their systems is not open to debate.

You can then use this expertise to continue your questioning further, using the **outside to inside questioning** approach to really explore the issues in more detail and enable the customer to create a compelling case for change.

WHAT TO FOCUS ON – ASSESSING THE ASSUMPTIONS

One of the key traits of the Transformational Seller is the ability to work with their customer to remove or further examine the assumptions that they are making and enable them to see the picture differently.

If you consider many of the challenges that you meet at all stages of the sales process and the objections and blockers that you have to overcome, most of these are based on customer assumptions.

These assumptions will be variations on themes such as:

- Everything's working fine.
- We have an existing provider.
- All providers are pretty much the same.
- Value for money means paying less.
- The risk is small, it's unlikely to affect us.

We will cover these assumptions in more detail and how to handle them in Chapter 14.

Exercise: Leveraging Your Expertise

In terms of leveraging your expertise and moving the customer through their buying journey, you can start to prepare in advance by considering:

- What are the frequent issues and challenges that customers raise?
- What assumptions are they making when raising these issues?
- What expertise can I bring to the conversation that will encourage the customer to re-examine the assumptions that they are making?
- What questions do I need to ask as part of the Set-Up to direct the customer towards the expertise I intend to deliver?
- What questions can I ask to reinforce the message and encourage the customer to explore further?

CHAPTER SUMMARY

- The Transformational Seller leverages their expertise to help guide the customer through their buying journey. They use it to explore the need for change, help the customer to develop their decision-making criteria (i.e., wish list), create a compelling business case and see it through to completion.

- The Transformational Seller's expertise derives from three sources; their **product knowledge, customer understanding** and **industry experience**.
- When knowledge is combined from these three sources it becomes true expertise:
- Product knowledge combined with industry experience provides **credentials**.
- Product knowledge combined with customer understanding creates **benefits**.
- Customer understanding combined with industry experience forms the basis for **value added expertise**.
- **Transformational Expertise** is the sweet spot where your Product Knowledge, Industry Experience and Customer Understanding combine to produce something particularly powerful and thought provoking for the customer.
- The approach that you use to 'deliver' your expertise to customers is important. Sellers and sales organisations often use the 'did you know' approach which doesn't engage the customer in the process or, worse still, tells them that their assumptions or assertions are wrong.
- To **leverage expertise**, we advocate the **SDE Approach**; the **set-up** involves asking questions to enable the customer to share their initial observations and thoughts; the **deliver** is where the seller introduces their observation and expertise; and the **explore** uses questions to encourage the customer to reflect on the implications of what they have learned.
- The use of questioning, like many other areas in the sales process, is pivotal to effectively leveraging expertise and creating buy-in from the customer.

- In establishing how and where to use your expertise, a useful starting place would be to examine the common assumptions that your customers make which often deflect them away from making positive decisions to change.

CHAPTER 11
MANAGING THE PROCESS

It isn't the mountains ahead to climb that wear you out, it's the pebble in your shoe.

Muhammed Ali

PUT A BELAY IN IT

Does this sound familiar? You had a really good meeting with your prospect: you established great rapport; you asked some insightful questions which opened up a need; their response was positive throughout and you left feeling that your chances of getting an order were extremely high. Three weeks later, the customer is still not responding to your increasingly desperate email or calls.

What happened? You didn't put a belay in!

The origins of the Belay Mountain Model

Bryn: Some years ago, I was discussing with some colleagues that seemingly 'great meeting' we have all been on at least once in our sales careers, the one where it ends up being the only time we ever met the client and we never hear from them again.

I was attempting to articulate why this happens and I needed to find a good analogy.

"What is it that a climber uses on their way up a mountain to stop themselves falling off?" I asked. No-one knew, not being mountaineers.

Fortunately, Google came to the rescue. The word I was looking for was 'belay'. Climbers use these to anchor themselves at various points along their ascent. If they subsequently stumble and fall it is never far, and they can then continue their progress to the summit.

My belay analogy suggested that winning an order is akin to climbing a mountain: the initial engagement starts at the base and there are usually numerous stages to negotiate before you reach the top, some harder to get over than others.

You need to climb the mountain as fast and skilfully as possible without falling off, beating other climbers (or competitors) to the top. Along the way you need to constantly assess what steps you have taken thus far, and plot what your next steps or route should look like.

The Belay Mountain Model is the glue in the sales process: it links the front end, the objectives a seller sets before the start of a meeting, to the commitments they gain at the back end. We'll explore the 'front end' of the process in more detail later in this chapter. When we discuss this concept with various sales teams, we ask them to share their typical objectives for a first customer meeting and then debate how far up the mountain they believe can be reached.

Typical answers include:

- Build good rapport with the client.
- Understand the client's main challenges.
- Find out more about the project, budget, authority, need and timeframe (BANT).
- Know who we are up against, potential advantages and disadvantages (CASE).
- Explain the benefits of working with us.

Whilst these activities, as we have already detailed in previous chapters, are all vital elements within the qualification and discovery process, they do not even get the seller as far as 'base camp' on their journey up the 'sales mountain'. All are important but none of these alone propel you up the mountain.

Usually during this exercise, a delegate will reply to the objectives question with something along the lines of "arrange another meeting" and the penny then will start to drop. Taking this further, we then ask: "What if you were able to get other stakeholders to that next meeting, or even if you are asked to present at your customer's next board meeting?" Can we climb even higher than that?

The point is that our objective for every interaction with the customer is to gain some form of **active commitment** and the more active the customer becomes, the better.

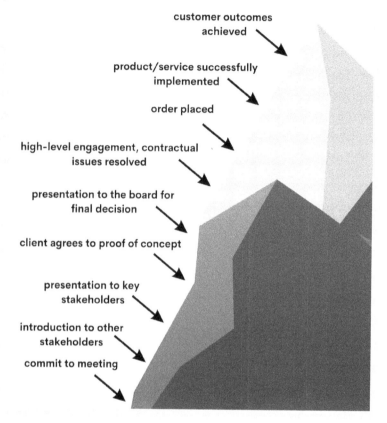

Figure 11.1: The Belay Mountain Model – Example Sales Journey

FIXING YOUR BELAYS – KEY POINTS TO CONSIDER

Always Present Your Proposal

We come across many sellers and organisations who are stuck in the habit of emailing quotations or proposals to their customers or prospects, without fixing any commitment or effort as to the next step on their *customer's* part. If the client asks for a proposal by tomorrow at 4pm, they will send it. If they then ask for this to be revised to fit their budget, they will amend it. If the client asks for specification modifications, they will change it. And so and so on. This is what we referred to previously as **The Labrador Effect**.

As a result, many of these proposals are often never given anything more than a cursory glance, the customer becomes difficult to get hold of, or they come back with a request for discount. Often the most common reason for 'business lost' recorded on the CRM system for these organisations is 'no response from the customer'.

One manufacturing company we worked with told us that their conversion rate was around three percent of quotations sent to orders won. They quoted for every enquiry that came their way. Can you imagine what a ninety-seven percent failure rate does to the morale of a sales team?

If a proposal or a quotation is required and is the next step in the process, then your customer agreeing to receive it does not require any activity on their part. To be active, they must commit to you presenting it, either in person or through a virtual meeting or call. This not only requires some degree of commitment on their behalf, but enables you to bring your solution to life, engage and ask questions of your customer, gain feedback and, perhaps most importantly, guarantees that it gets considered properly.

It's the ability to discuss, gain feedback and debate the content of your proposal with the customer, providing the opportunity for engagement and collaboration that creates the belay. Their ability to be involved in that process binds you just as the climber is bound to the rock.

Your Place or Mine?

Active commitment is a two-way street. The more that the client has to do as part of the next steps, the more effort that is involved, the more invested they are in seeing their buying journey through to completion.

This can be demonstrated with the difference between you meeting the customer in person or virtually or meeting a client at your offices instead of theirs.

The commitment required for a client to attend a meeting at *their* offices means they have to go into a meeting room for an hour (or even stay in their own office). However, if they come to see you, they are taking half a day or a day out of their busy schedule to travel often considerable distances which may include leaving home very early and / or returning late.

A client we have worked with who specialises in fuel testing for ships worldwide encourages potential customers to visit their laboratories. Given that these are dotted all over the world, this is a massive commitment for customers, and unsurprisingly, almost all who make that journey end up working with them. The visit often involves taking several days out of their busy week. It is highly unlikely that anyone would do that if they weren't serious about using their services.

We have tracked our own successes over the years and one thing stood out. Roughly four out of every five clients who came to see us at our offices ultimately bought from us.

Proof of Concept or the Free Trial?

For more technical businesses, we have seen how proofs of concept and free trials can carry a lot of weight within the decision-making process. However, these, too, are prone to potential issues with active commitment if the conditions of the trial are not stipulated and agreed up front.

The free trial that costs

Steve: We once worked with a client who provides highly specialist scientific equipment used in testing and analysis laboratories. They were very proud of the product quality. So much so, that it became de rigueur for sellers to offer a free trial to potential customers, confident that once they had used the product, there would be no going back.

In theory, this could have been a great example of active commitment. In order for the customer to use their product, they would need to go through a set-up, calibration and testing procedure which would equate to several hours work and then typically use it as part of their day-to-day business for several weeks.

The problem was that the free trial was offered without securing the commitment from the customer to use the product or review the outcomes. As a result, the sales director estimated that at any one time there were hundreds of thousands of pounds worth of stock gathering dust on customer's shelves that never got round to being trialled.

It had become the easy option for the sales team looking to gain a next step, often without creating a compelling need for change.

In offering any kind of trial or test, it's pivotal that the following questions are asked:

- Do you really need to offer this or is there a more positive next step you could take?
- What engagement has been agreed before, during and after the trial?
- What criteria has the customer agreed to measure the success of the trial against?
- What is the next step for the customer following the trial (assuming it meets their **success criteria**)?

Without the chance to consider these questions, there is a danger that the customer just goes through the motions with the trial. In other words, it is a trial suggested by the seller as a substitute for real commitment, and agreed to by the customer, because it's easier to go along with it if there's no compulsion to actually do anything 'active' on their part.

Getting a Customer Reference

One belay that seems to be used far too sparingly is the direct reference from an existing client. Companies may have plenty of testimonials and case studies on their websites, but these are far less powerful than your prospect speaking to one of your existing customers and understanding more about their experience of working with you.

Just as with your stories and examples, your prospect and your reference client don't necessarily need to be in the same sector: if the outcomes that they are striving for or the challenges they are seeking to solve are similar, this can still resonate powerfully.

Your prospect is looking for reassurance that selecting you is a sound and well-proven choice. No-one likes to be a guinea pig, and nobody enjoys making a bad selection decision, so the client reference goes a long way to making the customer feel comfortable, removing the FUD elements before making their commitment.

This is likely to become an increasingly useful tool in the New World. As collaboration becomes a more important part of a customer's decision-making criteria and the long-term partnership highly valued, so gaining insight into how you collaborate with others has increasing value. No-one sells you and your business like your best customers.

ASKING FOR COMMITMENT

Once again, 'mindset' plays a huge part in the belays you implement. Sellers often fail to gain active commitments, concerned they may be imposing on the customer or in danger of losing the cosy warm rapport they have built up. No-one likes to hear the word 'no'. Think about this for a minute: what is your prospect telling you if they won't meet with you again, are reluctant to introduce you to other stakeholders or are generally keeping you at arm's length?

They aren't that interested in working with you

Testing what your prospect will agree to is vital in managing your time and pipeline. You need to be bold but also realistic. Off the back of an initial discovery meeting, it is perhaps unlikely that the customer will invite you to present at their next board meeting. However, bringing other stakeholders and decision makers into the discussion is both realistic and feasible, with a view that the presentation to the board may happen further down the line.

PLAN AND EXECUTE

Returning to the **Plan** and **Execute** stages of the **SCOPE** Model, the more that you can work with your customer to map out the pivotal stages and lay out the belays in advance, the easier it will be to subsequently gain the necessary active commitment at each stage of the process. This will also significantly benefit forecast accuracy.

Scott versus Amundsen: a salutary lesson in planning ahead

The main reason that Roald Amundsen beat Robert Falcon Scott to the South Pole by a whole month was intense planning and preparation.

Firstly, Amundsen knew that too much sweat was their enemy as when it freezes, it causes immense pain. Therefore, his team moved slowly and wore loose clothing to allow the sweat to evaporate.

Also, Scott used brand new motorised sleds which Amundsen turned down as he knew they hadn't been tested in such harsh conditions. He was absolutely right as they broke down on the British expedition and – as Scott's ponies had died earlier – his team had to push the sleds themselves.

Scott had also only brought one tonne of supplies for seventeen men, on the assumption that he could locate supply depots along the way. However, due to the constant snow blizzards, Scott missed several depots in succession.

Amundsen, on the other hand, took three tonnes of supplies for five men. He could have missed every depot and still had enough supplies to go an extra 100 miles. Despite this, he wouldn't miss them. When he had established the locations of the depots, he strategically placed black flags where they were to avoid them getting lost in the snow.

When Amundsen and his team were safely home, Scott's team were still on their way back, having run out of supplies. Demoralised and exhausted they were ten miles from a supply store when, eight months later, their frozen bodies were found by a recoqnisance party.

Planning, preparation and most importantly, objective setting are all fundamental Transformational Seller activities. By setting clear and demanding goals for each step in the process, and by aiming to obtain active client commitments they:

- Begin with the end in mind.
- Know what they want to get out of each step in the process.

- Put belays in at each stage (i.e., create an 'active' next step).
- Control the process more assertively (thus avoiding The Labrador Effect).
- Aim high and bold each time, to speed the sales process up.

We will cover more about the 'how' of **gaining commitment** in Chapter 14 and you may also find it useful to refer to Chapter 8 and the SCOPE Model.

SHORT CUTS VERSUS TAKING THE LONG WAY ROUND

An issue that will challenge your collaborative skills in developing the plan and mapping out the belays may be the customer's lack of knowledge or the opaqueness of their own procurement processes. You may need to bring your expertise based on how other organisations have approached such decisions to work through the plan with the customer.

You need to strike the right balance between taking short cuts that derail the process, and the lengthier route consisting of additional steps that ultimately slow the process down, which require greater effort on both yours and the customer's part.

An example might be where the seller presents to a group of decision makers having only previously engaged with one of them or does so based on a brief provided without any discovery discussion. Conversely, we have seen sellers arrange a product trial or customer referral, when neither was necessary, because that's what they would normally do – an example of following a sales process rather than the buying journey.

Perhaps the most important aspect of all of this is being able to spot and adapt and, whatever the plan, flexing it accordingly.

Getting to the summit in record time

Bryn: My first sales role was selling artificial sports surfaces. We had a unique product which precluded the need for a base layer – our 'self-support system' saved considerable time and money.

I had a meeting with a community youth worker within a large local authority to discuss a multi-purpose dual-use pitch (dual-use meant shared education and community use).

Although I was the umpteenth supplier the youth worker had met, he really liked our product as they wanted to construct the facility quickly to minimise disruption at the school.

We discussed next steps, which included meeting the Chairman of Education to gain approval. If successful, we would present to the Education Committee, followed by final approval by the full council. This would take four to six months as they met infrequently.

"It's really important we move quickly if we are to undertake the construction in the school holidays. When realistically can we meet with the Chairman?" I asked, keen to get the next belay in.

"That's difficult, I'll have to liaise with his PA," he replied. "Hang on, though, what are you doing this lunchtime? He often has his lunch in the staff canteen on Thursdays".

I was a little hesitant: I didn't want to ambush such a key person during his lunch. However, it could be weeks before we meet.

Strike whilst the iron's hot, as they say. I therefore found myself being introduced to a man in a string-vest tucking into pie and chips who turned out to be the most influential person in the council. We talked over lunch and, he seemed keen on the idea.

"I need you to come and present to the rest of the Education Committee," he said. "We meet in a couple of months, unless of course, you are free at two o'clock this afternoon!"

Two months can be a long time in sales, so despite my lack of preparation, I found myself walking into the opulent council chambers, with twenty-odd council members there, armed only with my sports pitch sample, and gave my hastily prepared elevator pitch.

I called my boss from the phone in the room stating I needed a price for a three-court multi-purpose sports pitch immediately.

"You are joking, aren't you, Bryn?" he asked. When he realised that I wasn't, he called back in fifteen minutes with a rapidly calculated cost with enough margin to cover any surprises.

"What about discount?" asked the Chairman, once I'd presented the cost.

It was tempting to go back to my boss but having spent an hour or so in the meeting, I knew exactly what councillors would be tempted by, so I countered: "We don't know the site conditions or any issues we may encounter and so we're taking a huge risk here. We can't offer a discount, but we can arrange a press day when we start on site. We'll get you as Chairman, sitting in the digger to kick-start the project. After which we can host a food and drinks reception for you all and the press to celebrate this great project."

There then followed a succession of calls to directors of Planning, Recreation and Education, to sort out various 'minor details' such as planning permission for floodlights and getting around the normal lengthy tender process!
"What do you need from me now?" the Chairman said after this was concluded.

"An order would be good so we can get the site survey booked. I'm conscious that we want to be able to complete the work during the holidays."

"I can't give you that until after tonight, but I can give you a Letter of Intent to get you started. You write what you need form me and I'll sign it."

So, just a few hours after my initial meeting, I was hand-writing my own Letter of Intent for £92,000 on a sheet of headed council notepaper which the Chairman duly signed. The contract was signed the next day.

Whilst in this story there was a lot of luck involved with how everything dropped into place that day, it highlights a number of important points a seller needs to remember when managing the sales process:

- Mapping out the key steps enables you to recognise the importance of taking the chance to progress an opportunity faster.

- Securing active commitment from each stage is key, wherever you are at. It's about asking for commitment to the next step. Much of this is down to mindset. In the example in the story we gave, there was an opportunity for a quick win, and it was just too good not to take.

- If you have something that the customer really values, and can create urgency, then collaboration is the key to working together through the buying journey.

- When a client wants something urgently, they can often short-circuit the normal procurement process.

Exercise: The Belay Mountain Model

Using the Belay Mountain Model in this chapter, map the stages you normally need to work through from initial client engagement to securing the order.

Next, state what your typical objectives might be for each stage including what you need your client to agree to and what are the minimum and maximum objectives required to move up the mountain.

Apply this to a current opportunity that you are working on:

- What is the agreed next step?
- How much active commitment has been gained from the customer?
- What further commitment could have been obtained (that would have strengthened the belay further)?
- What are your objectives for the next step?

CHAPTER SUMMARY

- Just as mountaineers use **belays** to secure their ascent, so the Transformational Seller anchors themselves at various points throughout the sales process.
- Sales belays are based on **active commitment** from the customer. The more effort involved on their behalf, the more committed they are to working towards a solution and the more invested they are in seeing it through to completion.
- When a customer is reluctant to making any commitment, it's an indication that they aren't committed to following through the buying journey (or at least not with you).
- You should review your success ratios against the different belays that you use to identify which ones provide the greatest indicators of success.
- By getting clients to visit your offices, manufacturing plant, showroom or laboratory, they are effectively showing huge interest and your chances of winning the deal are significantly enhanced.
- Getting prospects to talk to one of your existing clients is incredibly powerful. No-one sells your company better than your best clients, and this greatly reduces the FUD elements for your prospect, enabling them to feel more comfortable in moving forward.
- You should ensure that after each stage you create a next step that genuinely moves you towards the order: you can waste a lot of time treading water with deals that get stuck.
- Flexibility combined with taking advantage of opportunities are the keys to success. Don't be too fixed

on having to follow your own sales process. Collaborate with your customer to come up with a plan to progress through the process together.

CHAPTER 12
PITCH PERFECT

That was a great supplier presentation.

I wish it had gone on for much longer!

No Customer Ever

When we consider 'pitching' we tend to think of slick Hollywood style presentations as seen in the series *Mad Men* with Don Draper using his imagination and creativity or in *The Pursuit of Happiness* with Will Smith's character Chris Gardner displaying honesty and humour.

The reality is very different, and usually consists of seemingly endless slide decks, flat, monotonous deliveries and rambling presenters. The result: sheer boredom.

The typical mistake made in sales pitches is to focus on the supplier and their products. As a result, they tend to be generic, they don't address the customer's explicit outcomes and they're often long and dull. Also, they tend to happen far too early in the process.

The Transformational Seller recognises that their pitch, when performed well, can make the crucial difference between winning and losing, particularly where there is limited differentiation between competing propositions.

Whatever the format of your pitch, the key elements which are central to creating an impact include:

- Creating a compelling opening.
- Developing win themes.
- Connecting through story-telling.
- The call to action.
- Engagement and collaboration.

It's worth remembering that whilst we refer here to the 'pitch', we could be referring to a formal stand-up presentation to an audience of decision makers, a one-to-one meeting to run through a proposal, a virtual meeting, a webinar presentation, a round table collaborative discussion, an off-the-cuff high level 'pitch' at the end of discovery or a product demonstration. A Transformational sale is likely to include several of these pitches, to different stakeholders and at different times during the sale.

CREATING A COMPELLING OPENING

"My name is Jack, I work for ABC, a leading workflow business in Bracknell established in 1984. We are a FTSE 500 company and were recently voted one of the UK's leading independent technology businesses. My presentation today is about the importance of workflow technology in business."

This opening is typical of the start of a pitch. It doesn't exactly get you on the edge of your seat! This style of opening is usually followed by slides that details company history, logos of prestigious customers and the ubiquitous map highlighting the company's global presence. Have a look at your own organisation's corporate pitch: there's a chance it could be very similar.

The first issue with this opening is simply that it's dull. No-one cares about how the company was formed, the historic timeline or the industry awards that they have won (at least not at this stage). The second issue is that it's all about the company and not about the customer. If the aim is to arouse excitement or passion, this opening fails immediately. It needs to be both *interesting* and *relevant* to the audience.

Opening a pitch is like making a prospecting call: you have an extremely short window in which to give your audience a reason to listen. How you open will vary depending on the situation; a more formal stand-up presentation to a larger audience verses a 1-2-1 pitch or demo may benefit from different approaches.

Your pitch can follow a similar format to the SCOPE Model for driving effective discovery. If you want to grab your customer's attention and interest, then you should open with what is important to them, which is their **success criteria** and their **challenges**. Whatever the format of your pitch and supporting material (slides, written proposal) the first element that the customer hears and sees from you should be about the customer, not you.

Pitch opening – an example

When we met last time, you discussed the company's goal of doubling in size over the next three years. In order to achieve this, you discussed the need to develop new product offerings that would enable you to expand into different vertical sectors.

Specifically, you stated that by 2025, you are targeting for at least fifty percent of your revenue to be in sectors outside of the oil and gas industry.

The challenges you face in opening these new markets from a design perspective include:

- *Reducing your run times down from the current six to eight-week timescales – enabling you to respond more effectively to customer requests.*
- *Dealing with more sophisticated and complex modelling.*
- *Mastering the design capability in-house – becoming less reliant on third party consultants to support the design process.*

I'm going to share with you some ideas and explore how best we can support you in achieving this.

Notice that at this stage there is no mention of the seller's products or credentials as these do little to establish their credibility. Showing the customer that you understand their success outcomes and their challenges will provide all the credibility you need at this stage.

OPENING A FORMAL PRESENTATION

Occasionally, you may be required to deliver a more formal pitch or presentation, possibly to a larger group. This changes the dynamics. In such cases, referring to the success criteria and challenges may be still appropriate, although they may have less impact for audience members who were not engaged in the discovery process.

In this case, you may wish to consider more formal ways of opening up and grabbing attention from the outset.

Such techniques could include:

A fact or quotation – a good fact, especially if shocking or different, can create a strong opener. However, these openings need to be relevant to your win themes and relate directly to your customer's success outcomes. One of our favourite openers was from a delegate who presented on the theme of 'The Need for Testing'. It went thus: "You don't need a working parachute to go sky-diving: but you do if you want to go more than once!"

A thought-provoking question – in Chapter 9 we showed the power that a single question can have in directing the thoughts of your audience or to grab attention. It can either be asked rhetorically or it can spark interaction and early-stage engagement.

Examples include:

- How much does a bad appointment cost your business?
- How do you increase performance by fifteen percent in just twelve months?

The question should link back to the themes and customer outcomes. Note how the second question here relates to a specific outcome that the customer may have stated.

Story or anecdote – if you choose to start your pitch with an anecdote, keep it brief. It can certainly create intrigue, prompting the audience to question the direction you are leading them in a similar way to how a good joke works. You must, however, tie it back into your central message.

We have seen this used to good effect. One example was a seller whose company offered fully integrated marketing solutions and told the story of spending hours working on a jigsaw only to find at the end one of the pieces was missing. She linked the frustration of this experience to having one of the pieces of your marketing solution missing.

DEVELOPING THE 'WIN THEMES'

Creating a winning theme

Bryn: Years ago, I sold health and fitness equipment to local authority leisure centres. At the time, sunbeds were popular as they took up minimal space and generated significant round-the-clock income. There was one major problem though. This was the safety issues connected with over-use. We have all seen the 'Tangerine Tanner'!

One opportunity saw me pitching against the two market leaders, either of which would have been an easy option for the customer. I knew I needed to do something different if I was to win the contract and give the customer confidence in spending public money on something that was getting a lot of bad press.

With this in mind I came up with the theme: Creating a Centre of Excellence for Safer Tanning.

Instead of focusing on the product, my pitch centred on providing training to their staff around safer tanning and managing usage to ensure individuals didn't overdo it. The aim was to create a carefully monitored service that would still provide a great source of revenue.

Moving away from the traditional product pitch felt like a gamble, but under the circumstances, I had nothing to lose. However, I was disappointed at the end of my presentation by the muted response I received.

The following morning the client called with the news they were awarding my company the contract. It turns out they loved the idea of becoming the first Centre of Excellence for Safer Tanning in the UK. I had taken their silence for indifference. In reality they were quietly absorbing the idea which they then discussed very enthusiastically afterwards.

When reflecting on my sales career, I regret not taking this bolder approach a lot more often.

Creating a great win theme starts with the questions:

- What outcomes is the customer looking to achieve by partnering with us?
- What is different about what we are proposing?
- What challenges are the customer aiming to overcome?

Tailoring your themes to match the stated outcomes and challenges from the Discovery Phase plus your differentiators means your pitch is truly customer-centric and engaging.

Figure 12.1: Developing the Win Themes

Developing customer-centric win themes

Bryn: We once worked with a major Insurance company creating and delivering engaging presentations to IFAs (Independent Financial Advisors) who were, in effect, their sales channel.

We kicked off by reviewing their typical presentation:

"We have a long-standing reputation since being established in 1893... we get involved in sports sponsorship... you will have seen our advertisements on TV... we are one of the leading Insurance ..."

We told them to stop before they even finished their opening and asked them why would we care about any of this? We told them to imagine they were running a small business with all the issues that a typical IFA faces. We asked them to think about what would really matter to them in that situation. The key question would be: "What are we trying to achieve and what's getting in the way?"

We tasked delegates to step into their customer's shoes and work on coming up with some questions. Out of the discussions, three core questions that a customer would need to ask emerged:

- **Can you keep us safe?** With strict regulatory guidelines from the FCA (Financial Conduct Authority) constantly evolving, how can you support us in staying on top of the changes? We can't afford to fall foul of them and potentially lose our license.

- **Are you easy to deal with?** We want to avoid having to 'jump through hoops' when we send you an application and minimise time spent on administration. We need transparency for your acceptance criteria, and to work with us to resolve client enquiries and claims. Issues with service reflect badly on us and take up too much of our time.

- **Will you reward us fairly and quickly?** We are a small business and cash flow is critical. It's important to know we'll get our commissions paid fairly and on time.

We now had the core themes for their presentations (as well as the title slide):

Safer, Easier and More Rewarding

Connecting Through Story-Telling

We have seen an explosion in recent years of the culture of the 'review'. Trip Advisor, Airbnb and Amazon all use customer reviews to support and drive purchasing decisions. The reason why they are so valuable goes back to the principle of FUD factors and the need to take away some of the uncertainty (or sometimes raise it) that comes with making a purchasing decision.

Despite customer reviews becoming an integral part of B2C buying experiences, many areas of the B2B world have yet to fully embrace them. Often a seller's knowledge is limited with little being organised or shared amongst their own team around case studies or proofs. Providing evidence of success, specific to a project your customer is embarking upon, significantly de-risks their decision and provides confidence in their choice of supplier; it's the 'buy IBM' principle we talked about in Chapter 3.

If you are to use a case study, it needs to be relevant. We have often seen sellers citing examples from the same sector as the one they are working in assuming that this automatically makes them good examples. For instance, pitching to a small family firm of accountants and describing the system you put in place for KPMG or PWC won't resonate.

Secondly, you should consider the mechanism by which the case study is delivered. Bringing it to life through the medium of story-telling enables the customer to develop an emotional connection. It's not the sector that creates the connection, nor the recognition of the company name. The connection goes back to what matters to the customer; their outcomes and challenges. Your story or case study needs to highlight this. If you can demonstrate the case of a customer who had the same desired outcome or similar challenges to your current customer, the sector becomes less relevant.

The quality that makes a great story or reference is how much it mirrors the emotional journey that you are taking your customer through.

You should start with your case study's desired outcomes, share their frustrations and pains, demonstrate the relief or security you provided and the determination that the customer demonstrated in achieving their desired results.

When structuring your stories, which can be used not only at various stages throughout your pitch, but throughout the entire sales process, you will benefit from basing your structure around classic traditions of story-telling.

Any classic story can be distilled down into the following elements:

- Quest – what the central character of the story sets out on.
- Conflict – the barriers and challenges in their way.
- Action – what the central character does to overcome these barriers.
- Conclusion – the quest is complete and the result is achieved.

QUEST   CONFLICT   ACTION   RESULT

Figure 12.2: Structure of Sales Stories

The most important element of story-telling is that if you want your story to resonate with your prospect, you need to make the customer in the story the central character not you, your company or your product. Your offering is the tool that the 'customer' used to successfully complete their quest.

To make it engaging, the 'customer' doesn't need to be in the same industry as your prospect – they just need to be on a similar quest or be facing similar challenges.

THE CALL TO ACTION

The end of your pitch needs to include a **call to action**. Put simply, this is what you want your customer to do as a result of your pitch. The ultimate call to action is that the customer agrees to the sale and you close it right there. That seldom happens at this stage, except potentially for more transactional sales. In the New World this will be rare.

The greatest failing of most sales pitches (aside from being boring) is that the call to action isn't well prepared. The seller ends up 'winging it' when it comes to closing the pitch and this results in poor next steps and constant chasing up of the client or awaiting their call.

If you have conducted your discovery utilising the SCOPE Model, you should have built up your backward plan which outlines the next steps. Of course, this plan depends upon your key contacts and their understanding of what needs to happen to move forward. The next step after the pitch is to create a call to action from your audience.

Imagine that from your discovery meeting you established that if the pitch went well, the next step would be to gain board approval. You established that board meetings were generally a closed-shop, and it would be highly irregular to have a potential supplier present at them.

Your call to action following the pitch should therefore be to have all stakeholders to be fully supportive and confident in presenting your proposal to the board. To achieve this, you need to make sure that they are given the opportunity to discuss any elements of the proposal they don't like, aren't relevant or were missed. This will mean that you have a chance to rectify the situation there and then.

Questions you should look to ask:

- From what you have seen, how confident are you that our solution will enable you to achieve your outcomes?
- How comfortable are you in putting this in front of the board?
- What additional points would you like further clarity on?

Then you can position the next step and before presenting this to the board you can ask:

- Which elements will resonate most with the board?
- What possible reservations, if any, do you think the board might have?
- What else do you think the board needs to hear or see to be convinced?

Note how this second strand of questions asks how the client believe others (i.e., members of the board), will perceive the proposal. By using the third-party approach, it is now easier for the stakeholders to raise their own issues and concerns that may otherwise have gone unsaid.

You are now able to offer further clarity, either immediately, at a further meeting or call prior to the next step. The main thing is that it's not being left to chance.

GAINING FEEDBACK AND GENERATING DIALOGUE

One question we ask sellers is: "If you have set aside an hour for the pitch, how long should your presentation be?"

This issue isn't usually given much thought. The content of most sales pitches is based around what the seller would like to say rather than how long they have to say it. As a result, sellers often fail to nail the call to action, and the presentation ends up being rushed at the end. However, the final stage is where a lot of the 'real' selling happens. It's the time when the seller and the customer can engage in two-way communication.

In a conventional pitch, gaining feedback can be challenging. Many sellers find this uncomfortable (remember that if it feels uncomfortable then you should probably do it!). If they believe that the pitch went well, they would rather walk away feeling good than risk of being told otherwise (just like the ostrich). If they feel it went badly, they don't want that reinforced by the customer.

The main reason it's challenging though, is because the seller makes it challenging.

The most common, and ironically, least effective, way of getting feedback is to ask: "Are there are any questions?" Here, you are putting in a condition that feedback has to come in the form of a question. Furthermore, conscious that their colleagues (and perhaps bosses) are present, they may feel pressured into ensuring that their question is an intelligent one – or at least not a stupid one. Faced with this, many people stay silent.

Better to ask the customer for their thoughts and observations. With this approach, there are no restrictions as to how the customer needs to present their feedback and it becomes easier for them to articulate their thoughts. However, this method isn't fool proof. The customer may still be reluctant to provide feedback because you haven't convinced them yet. Or it could be that the dynamic between different members of the audience means that individually they are reluctant to go out on a limb without having gained consensus.

Alternatively, they may be following procurement protocols, conscious not to give anything away until they have evaluated the competition (which is usually a good reason to be the final company presenting). This should never prevent you from asking of course, because the dialogue you create here is potentially the most important part of the pitch and should be carefully planned to ensure that you can drive the call to action that you need.

Returning to the question of how long the pitch should be, when considering the questions and their subsequent exploration, it's clear that allowing between five and ten minutes at the end is inadequate. It is better to use the 20:40:40 structure for allocating time. Each portion represents the percent of time that should be spent on opening, message and closing the pitch, respectively.

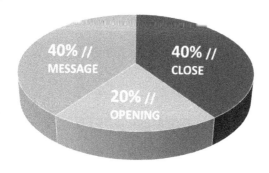

Figure 12.3: The 20:40:40 Structure for Pitching

It's during this last forty percent (the 40 at the end of 20:40:40) at the end of the pitch that you can really get your customer collaborating through debate around how they see the product or service working, what they particularly like about it and what they think about options or alternatives (to drive greater ownership of the solution). This will help you together to tailor the solution.

THE TAKEAWAYS

It takes considerable effort to shift someone's thinking, especially if they have not perceived an issue with the way they currently operate. For instance, from our observations the majority of people aren't totally happy with their current bank, but how often do they change banks?

So, the key takeaways at the end of a pitch need to be powerful and should make the audience ponder the following questions:

- What am I doing currently that really needs to change?
- What are the potential consequences if I don't make that change?
- What opportunities could exist if I do make the change?
- What if I make the wrong choice of supplier or base my decision on price?
- Why do I need to make this change sooner rather than later?

ENGAGEMENT AND COLLABORATION

If you're a sports fan, or a music lover, you'll appreciate the benefits of watching a match or a concert in the comfort of your own home – no queues for the toilets, no over-priced refreshments, no risk of getting wet in the rain or waiting for hours to get off the car park. All these factors lead to watching at home providing a better experience than being at the event.

Yet we still would rather be live at the event than at home. Why? Because when you are there, you are more than just a passive observer, you are involved. Your cheers (Bryn – Liverpool) or jeers (Steve – Stoke City) can be heard by the protagonists, and together with thousands of strangers, you are somehow influencing the eventual outcome. When the lead vocalist holds out the microphone at a concert for the audience to sing the chorus, they are no longer listening to the music, they're performing it. In other words, they're collaborating.

Collaboration is key to what makes a good Transformational Seller. Encouraging the customer to be actively involved in the pitch is equally as vital. This isn't just through questions, but by metaphorically handing the customer the microphone. Throughout your pitch you should ask them to elaborate on their thoughts, their reactions to your key points and tell you how they feel your solution will enable them to achieve their outcomes.

Furthermore, consider how you can get them actively involved in the development of your solution. Using every opportunity, you can to gain customer input into the solution, such as providing them with options to discuss or exploring issues with you during the pitch, is the very definition of collaboration.

The more your customer is *involved*, the more their interest is retained, the better the feedback you get and, most importantly, the more emotionally invested they become in your solution.

Aristotle's Rules of Engagement

Aristotle, one of the greatest philosophers of all time, talked about the three proofs which evidenced a persuasive speaker:

- **Ethos** – character and reputation
- **Pathos** – emotional appeal
- **Logos** – logic

A persuasive message, he said, uses all three proofs in tandem and the goal is to move the audience from Point A to B. Over 2,300 years later, his principle still applies.

Ethos involves trust, credibility and sincerity, all critical traits of a Transformational Seller, and we are hard-wired to notice when these are faked.

Pathos relates to the emotions felt by the audience. Aristotle believed these needed to be stirred for people to be persuaded (see Why You Should Give Up Smoking at the end of this chapter).

Logos, Aristotle said, was concerned with the content – the choice of words, stories and evidence to back up the other two attributes.

THE UBIQUITOUS DEMO

A rising phenomenon in the sales world, particularly for tech companies and SaaS businesses, is the demonstration or **demo**. It's a specific form of pitch the aim of which is to enable the customer to visualise and immerse themselves in what it's like to own the product.

The concept is simple – let's show you how our product works, how easy it is to use and how good it looks. This will create a desire to buy. It's not a new principle – infomercials have been running on television for years. Before then the vacuum cleaner sellers would come to your home and attempt to wow you with the capability of their product.

There's no doubt that a demonstration of your product can add real value to the Transformational Sales approach, only if it follows the same rules as any other form of pitch or proposal.

- A **demo** needs to be personalised and tailored to the customer outcomes. Demos are often product-centred and focus too much on demonstrating as many product features as possible. If you haven't conducted an effective discovery, then the demo that follows can only be generic and feature led.
- Less is more. As with any pitch, the demo should focus on your core win themes that combine the customer's stated outcomes, your differentiators and their problems or issues. You don't always need the details of how your software does it – you just need to emphasise the end result that the customer can expect.
- The demo is not a tutorial. There is a danger that the demo turns into a 'how to' session, where the sales executive takes the audience through how to perform certain tasks or actions step-by-step. It's worth bearing in mind that those who have the authority to make decisions on software are often not the same people as those that will use it. Tutorials are for the users after the software has been purchased. A client of ours who sells complex simulation software for engineering firms often warns their sales team: "If you're talking about nodes and elements, you're talking to the wrong person."
- Your product is nowhere near as interesting as you think (it's a bit like somebody else's holiday photos). The customer is interested in the net result and the product is just a means to an end.
- Engagement and attention are difficult to maintain when you are watching someone else perform tasks on

a screen, particularly when it is being delivered remotely (and the customer can be completing all kinds of other tasks whilst you are demonstrating). Using software is not a spectator sport, so if you can't physically involve the customer in using or playing with the software, then you need to consider how else you maintain engagement. Remember, the more the customer is involved in discussions and making decisions (i.e., the more collaboration within your demo), the more ownership they will take for helping drive the sale forward.

Many businesses have focused on making the demonstration the core part of their sales process and look to progress this at an early stage because they see it as the quickest route to the sale. In addition, streamlining the demo process and even having specific people whose sole role in the sale is to deliver the demo, feels like a great way to standardise the sales process and hence make it scalable. Standardisation and scalability, whilst attractive to many businesses in growth phase, have a tendency to lead to Transactional Selling.

Whilst this might not deter businesses from doing it, after all, if you chuck enough mud at the wall some will stick, it does present two major issues.

- **Issue one** – adoption rates following the sale may be low and, where based on subscription or even pay per use, the profitability of many deals may not be realised.
- **Issue two** – as a sales professional, generic product-led demos are perhaps one of the easiest things for the selling organisation to automate, leaving your skills at delivering a slick demo redundant.

NEXT STEPS

Having created the desire for change through your questioning, customer engagement and in leading the emotional journey, you may feel that you are only a short step away from gaining commitment. However, as our understanding of the customer buying journey supports, there are still some hurdles to overcome before a deal is won and we can start delivering outcomes for the customer. Ironically, it's at this point where too many sellers take a back seat and leave the sales process to manage itself through to the close.

The next two chapters look at how the traditional sales concepts of negotiation and overcoming objections need significant re-engineering in the New World and how the Transformational Seller collaborates with their customer through the latter stages of their buying journey.

Speaking from the heart: Why You Should Give Up Smoking

Bryn/Steve: We witnessed a remarkable example of persuasion and impact when running a Pitching Skills Programme in Dallas (which, as we said in the introduction, was where we first conceived the idea for this book). The delegates were Taxation specialists who needed to promote their services, so pitching was an important skill for them to learn.

Many of the delegates had real trepidation around attending: glossophobia, the fear of public speaking affects up to seventy-seven percent of people, so we had anticipated this, especially from a group who were, by profession, accountants. One such delegate arrived visibly shaking and admitted she had considered not showing up.

To ease them into the programme we broke them into smaller groups to work on delivering a short 'lifestyle pitch' on a topic they felt passionate about. The extremely nervous delegate stood up, but determined to conquer her fears chose: 'Why You Should Give Up Smoking'. For the next ten minutes she had the whole room absolutely spellbound whilst she talked about her father's lung cancer and how he could no longer even manage a short walk with his own grandchildren. This was the same immensely strong father of her youth, she explained, who used to carry her on his back across any terrain.

By the time she'd finished, there wasn't a dry eye in the house. Her passion for the subject, the love for her father and her fear of loss was so compelling, convincing and memorable. It was also effective. We noticed that many of the smokers in the room declined the opportunity for a cigarette break following her speech.

It seems that she achieved her call to action without even asking!

Exercise 1: Developing Win Themes

For a recent pitch you have delivered, or one that you have coming up, review the following:

- What outcomes were your customer attempting to achieve?
- What problems were they facing that were potentially making the achievement of their outcomes more difficult?
- How does you offering differ from the alternatives that they were reviewing?

From the answer to thee three questions, look at how they might combine to create an overarching win theme (or themes) that could be the mainstay of your pitch.

Exercise 2: Creating stories

Identify a success story, case study or example that you could include as part of your pitch. Using the four-stage structure of quest, conflict, action and result, create a story where your customer is the central hero (and your products or services are merely the tool they used).

Aim for the story to be no more than two- to three-minutes long and ensure that you and your company don't inadvertently become the hero.

Once confident with this structure, you can start to create a bank of stories that cover off different customer quests and conflicts – ensuring you have a relevant story for every occasion.

CHAPTER SUMMARY

- Many pitches start off by boring the customer with facts about the seller's organisation, their history, products and services. Better to grab the customer's attention using questions, quotations or anecdotes to create interest or intrigue.
- When pitching or presenting proposals, sellers place too much emphasis on their own products and services and not enough on what matters to the customer (i.e., their stated outcomes).
- Developing a Transformational pitch starts with reviewing what the specific outcomes will be for the customer as a result of working with the seller.
- The Transformational pitch will be based around the development of a series of win themes. These will combine the key elements of the seller's proposition (their differentiators or key selling points), the

customer's outcomes and the challenges or issues that are impacting their achievement of these.

- Stories or case studies often miss the mark because they fail to establish a relevant emotional connection to the customer's outcomes and the issues they are facing. These stories should aim to mirror aspects of the customer's world and enable the customer to connect with the central character of the story.
- The **call to action** is the most important, and yet often the most rushed and poorly executed part of the pitch.
- To secure a **call to action** the Transformational Seller needs sufficient time for feedback and dialogue. The **20:40:40 structure** is recommended for mapping out the different phases of the pitch.
- The importance of collaboration through customer engagement during the pitch cannot be overstated and you should take every opportunity to ensure that your audience is involved throughout the pitch, rather than them being passive observers.

CHAPTER 13
A GAME BOTH TEAMS CAN WIN

Let us never negotiate out of fear. But let us never fear to negotiate.

John F. Kennedy

NEGOTIATION GAME THEORY

Most people fear losing. It evokes feelings of rejection, disappointment and failure, which is why 'zero-sum' sports tend to result in ecstatic winners and distraught losers. Your co-authors share a passion for cricket, which frequently bucks this trend: it can be played over five days for six hours a day and still result in a draw: try explaining the appeal of that to an American!

In the same way, the customer buying journey can carry on, not just for days, but months or even years and still sometimes conclude without a result.

As the customer continues on their buying journey to the later phases of **resolve concerns** and **commit to act** it is likely that both parties will start to engage in negotiation, the process by which the details of what will be exchanged from one party to the other will become defined and agreed.

The possible results from a negotiation are often talked about in terms of:

- One side wins the other side loses: win-lose
- Both sides lose: lose-lose
- Both sides win: win-win

The third outcome dictates that a good negotiation should achieve a result not possible in sport, in that both teams can win. The achievement of these outcomes depends upon the approach that each party takes:

> **Collaboration versus Competition**
> **Capitulation or Coercion**

In the New World, suppliers and customers increasingly need to work together as partners to ensure mutual survival. (Note, whilst most customers like to negotiate, they don't want their suppliers to go bust.) **Fostering collaboration**, one of the three core pillars of Transformational Selling, therefore becomes a critical part of the negotiation approach.

Whilst the collaborative approach has been espoused for many years, the backdrop to most negotiation training remains wedded to Game Theory and the idea of winners and losers using a more coercive and competitive approach.

Sellers are told:

- You should be collaborating with customers to achieve win-win scenarios.
- It's about building a strong, mutually beneficial business relationship.
- Ask questions to understand what's really important to your customer.

Whilst simultaneously being advised to:

- Avoid giving too much information away.
- Suggest your variables are costly, so that your customer's perception is that they are of high value.
- Take your time in giving a response – agreeing something too quickly suggests to the other party that you are either desperate or that it's easy for you to offer.
- Go in a bit higher to give you room to offer a discount and still achieve the standard price.

Can you see the paradox here? You can't genuinely collaborate with the customer whilst continuing to play games, withhold information or be economical with the truth.

In the New World, the competitive game playing side of negotiation will still exist, but it will sit within those sales conditions at the Transactional end of the spectrum. However, at the Transformational end, the traditional negotiation paradigm needs to change. This is because the **resolving concerns** stage of the buying journey is no longer about the mechanics of the transaction but about the process of creating a genuine working partnership.

As part of this process The Transformational Seller will need to:

- Operate in a more collaborative way.
- Guide the customer as to the best way to collaborate.

DEFINITION OF WINNING AND LOSING

At what point does anyone win in a negotiation? Is it when you get everything that you want, most of what you want, or enough of what you want?

Do you automatically lose when a deal falls through, or is that an over-simplification? If a deal dies due to lack of agreement, it potentially means that your product or service is still available to someone else.

The Transformational Seller needs to question why they are negotiating. Frequently the negotiation is driven by the customer 'trying to get the best price' and the seller 'aiming to get the best deal', often underpinned more by ego than business necessity.

This strategy focuses on the wrong things when defining 'winning and losing'. The focus should be on the 'outcomes' for both parties, and the ultimate outcomes not simply the negotiation outcomes (i.e., price and terms).

Did we win?

Imagine the following scenario:

You negotiate to sell your product or service for £50,000. You had to go below the price you quoted to help your customer strengthen the business case internally. It still equates to a decent margin (say twenty percent) that's above the average GP (gross profit) that your company had targeted. It makes a good contribution to the profit targets for the company and your own quota.

Did you win?

On the face of it you did. However, the customer, by implementing your product was able to solve a problem that then enabled them to make over £1,000,000 in additional profit (compared with the £10,000 profit that your business made). The customer could have paid multiple times over and still made an enormous return on investment. So, they obviously won.

Do you still think that you won as well?

The answer now depends upon what perspective you take. You may feel that as part of your discussions, your customer was not open with you as to the size of the problem that you were solving and was underhand on getting you to agree to a discount, knowing the potential difference it could make.

Of course, the customer could argue that you were also slightly underhand by quoting an initial price above what you needed to achieve.

And yet this is how most negotiations are conducted and how most business relationships start. Indeed, both parties would have stated that they were aiming for a win-win, but was that really the case and were they genuinely collaborating?

We will start by looking at the three typical negotiation results, why they occur and how we can create true collaboration with customers as part of the negotiation.

RESULT ONE – WIN-LOSE

Whilst sellers rarely admit it, often they accept a situation where the customer gets virtually everything they demand in return for the order. Negotiation is driven by coercion. Fear of losing the business drives seller behaviours. In other words, the seller is concerned that the customer might opt for a cheaper competitor or that the budget might not get approved. This often happens at the first sign of customer reservations and can impact the price agreed and the overall service offering.

We have frequently observed sellers say to customers:

- Yes fine, we can include that in the contract.
- That's no problem, we'll make that fit into your budget.
- You need a faster response time; we can arrange that at no extra cost.

They do this without fully appreciating the ramifications of what they are agreeing to, or how this could impact their business in terms of the order process; production scheduling; logistics; software development programs; disruption to other projects; and worst of all, the margin attained.

This often represents a no-way-back scenario for the ongoing relationship. The servant-master paradigm becomes fixed and hard to change. Having caved once, the customer is likely to demand more from you next time.

Capitulation has unfortunately become the norm for many transactional businesses where margins are already tight. The seller, often lacking the sales skills and mindset, feels obliged to acquiesce to the demands of their customer with the stated concern that, 'otherwise they will go elsewhere'. Besides which they have targets to hit!

Perversely, when we ask sellers why customers buy from them, they almost invariably cite the *strength of the relationship*, which, if it is genuinely strong, could surely not be broken that easily purely by the lure of a cheaper price.

The question to ask is whether this is a *win* for either party. Typically, if one side has felt coerced into the deal, through fear of loss or some form of deception, then the 'win' for other side tends to be short-lived.

If the customer has worn down a supplier to get them to offer a big discount, they may find that the after sales service and customer support received reflects this. In the same way, if a supplier has used an advantageous position to coerce the customer into accepting a deal (such as a being specified, supply shortages, or other forms of 'compulsion'), then the customer may be more difficult to satisfy and make an issue of any minor discrepancy in service or quality. The relationship is unlikely to be beneficial for either party long term.

Avoiding customer resentment

Bryn: We worked with a FTSE 100 company who needed to put their prices up substantially to their retail customers. Most of their products were purchased in dollars and, when exchange rates went dramatically south, to balance out the exchange rate losses they stood to lose over sixty percent of their annual profit if they didn't increase prices substantially.

There was a huge fear amongst their sellers around how their customers would react. We focused on the importance of explaining the situation transparently.

As market leaders, the customer service they offered was unrivalled in the industry and was highly valued. Therefore, the choice was either to strip this back considerably or invoke the price increase.

By taking an honest, open and direct approach outlining the reasons for the increase and the options, whilst simultaneously questioning to re-establish their customer's most important aspects of the service, they fostered a collaborative approach that enabled them to gain agreement to the increase to ninety-two percent of their customers.

This, combined with some other measures, ensured that they were able to maintain their desired profitability and previous service levels to their customer base.

RESULT TWO - LOSE-LOSE

Historically the idea of two parties failing to reach agreement has been described as a lose-lose scenario. However, this is something of a misnomer. A lose-lose often occurs where both parties have been unable to coerce the other on one or more aspects of a deal. However, if either party is attempting coercion, we need to ask, is this really the basis for a good working relationship? Sellers fear a 'walk away' scenario, because it represents the potential loss of an opportunity that they may have been working on for some time, which is why there is always a temptation to capitulate and gain something from all the effort expended.

In Chapter 5, we gave the example of an earth-moving equipment company which discounted heavily on new machines, leaving their margin in a precarious state. Work on their skills and mindset provided them with the courage to walk away from deals which didn't make financial sense, many of which they subsequently secured at a more profitable rate, enabling them to virtually double their margins and get the business back on track.

Whilst this can appear to be a risky strategy, it is an essential one. What was interesting in this case was the way in which the sellers had that conversation. The threat of walk-away can sound like coercion ('accept our terms or the deal is off'), but in reality, they shared their situation with the customer. They explained *why* they had to maintain a certain margin and when they did this, customers often responded positively. A seminal moment was when a customer said: "I was always going with you, I just wanted to see how far I could push you."

Prepared to walk away

Bryn: In my mid-twenties I became a partner in an IT recruitment business, joining a more experienced colleague. I had secured a great meeting with the Head of Recruitment for a major telecommunications company based in the south, requiring a five-hour drive.

When we arrived, we were ushered into the customer's spacious office where the customer sat on a leather swivel chair behind his large oak desk, leaving us perched on small uncomfortably hard chairs. He had many vacancies to fill, and his opening gambit was to say that the maximum he would pay for any placement was fifteen percent of base salary. We typically charged between twenty and twenty-five percent.

Even years later, I vividly remember what happened next. My business partner rose from his chair, put his notepad in his briefcase, shook the customer's hand and said: "Well, Mike, I'm not sure there's a lot here to discuss. I'm afraid that we're not going to be able to work together on that basis." Then he turned to leave. I was dumfounded. For a few seconds I remained seated thinking of the huge effort I'd put into setting up this meeting, the long drive home, all for nothing. I felt angry with my business partner, but realised I had no choice but to follow him.

We were almost out of the door when Mike responded: "Wait a second, can't we discuss this further?"

An hour later we signed exclusive terms on several roles. It was a gutsy call from my colleague and a lesson learned by his wide-eyed protégé.

Over the years, we have found that standing your ground can actually *increase* your chances of getting a sale.

One thing worth noting is the recognition of any aspects of your offering, or your customer's expectations, that could become sticking points in the negotiation phase. It is better to broach these early in the conversation to ascertain the degree of flexibility. This includes the concept of price.

When to Talk Price

Conventional wisdom dictates that you should avoid talking about price until you have built the need, sold the benefits and gained the customer's buy-in as to why your solution solves their pains and enables them to achieve their desired outcomes. There's a logic to this. The customer may be immediately put off by the price without you having had the opportunity to build value.

However, whilst holding off or stalling on the price conversation might work for shorter sales cycles or buying journeys, it's invariably a problem for multi-stage sales processes. Invariably a Transformational sale takes a commitment from both parties to spending time on the Discovery Phase, potentially with several stakeholders, developing quotations, preparing presentations and proposals, attending pitches and demonstrations and often in-depth fact-finding and analysis. All in all, there should be a significant investment from both parties, and the Transformational Seller consequently needs to ensure that the opportunity 'has legs' before committing their time and resources to the opportunity.

In particular, and as part of the Level 1 – BANT qualification, you should be ascertaining the potential budget for the programme, ensuring that it is realistic, bearing in mind the outcomes the customer needs to achieve. Often the customer may not have a budget, particularly where the seller has created the initial interest through highlighting a compelling event or eroding satisfaction levels. In such cases, the customer will need to find the necessary funds and therefore you should consider the importance of testing out the budget at an early stage.

You may need to consider this as part of the initial discovery, weaving it into the Options or Plan aspects of the SCOPE

Model, to manage expectations and establish whether your solution is a viable option before investing huge amounts of time and resource into an opportunity that may never reach fruition.

RESULT THREE - WIN-WIN

Transformational Collaboration

The Transformational Seller, by **leveraging expertise**, **fostering collaboration** and **focusing on outcomes** puts themselves in a strong position to gain the customer's trust and create a true partnership.

A question you may ask at this stage is: "What if my customer isn't interested in a partnership?"

In that case it's worth asking:

- How much value is there to be gained in working with a customer who wishes to maintain a master-servant relationship?
- What have you done to challenge the customer's mindset around their desire for a master-servant a partnership?
- Are you better off building a base of customers who recognise the value in what you are able to offer and how this helps them to achieve their business outcomes?

COLLABORATIVE NEGOTIATION THROUGH SCOPE MODEL

The prisoner's dilemma

The prisoner's dilemma is used in Game Theory. The premise is that two suspects are detained separately for a series of crimes that they have committed together. The evidence against both is weak and requires a confession. Each of them is offered a deal to 'rat' the other one out, in return for a reduced sentence.

The best outcome is that they both stay silent, but this is risky. If one remains silent and the other talks, the first is likely to receive a much stiffer sentence, hence there's a strong temptation to be the one who confesses first.

It's a classic example of a situation where two individuals, acting in their own self-interests, fail to achieve as good an outcome as one where they collaborate.

For true collaboration to occur, the Transformational Seller approach needs to be one of transparency, as does that of the customer. The seller has to first outline the 'rules' of engagement, and then guide the customer through the process.

SCOPE MODEL FOR COLLABORATIVE NEGOTIATION

To assist with this, we return to the SCOPE Model introduced during the Discovery Stage. This time, we can use it, with some adaptions, as basis for the collaborative negotiation.

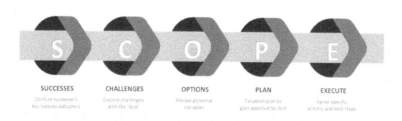

Figure 13.1: SCOPE Model – For Collaborative Negotiation

Successes – Confirm customer's key success outcomes

During the discovery we explored what the customer's success criteria looked like (note, that when we talk about 'customer success criteria', we mean their aims by working with us, not the price they are aiming to achieve through negotiation!). We open the Negotiation Phase by going back to these success criteria, reconfirming them but also now stating our own.

The customer's focus is around achieving a set of results or outcomes, whilst for a seller, it is likely to be achieving a profitable deal, and a longer-term relationship providing a fair return for the effort expended. If the customer is specific around the metrics and results that they need to achieve, in the spirit of collaboration, then as sellers we should also be specific about ours.

Challenges – Explore the challenges with the 'deal'

Having reviewed and agreed the success criteria, we can now explore the challenges for both parties within the deal. We can ask whether the challenges relate to price or any other aspects.

The important element here is that both parties need to explain *why*. If the customer wants a discount, the seller needs to ask *why* the current price is a challenge for them. It may be that it exceeds the budget allocated or prevents them from being able to invest in other projects, or that it would require another level of authorisation for sign off.

The key here is to encourage the customer to share their motives. However, it is important that the seller also declares their motives. Just as the customer should explain their rationale for a discount, so the seller should explain their rationale for wanting to protect the price.

Options – Review potential variables

Within any deal there will be a range of 'variables' to discuss. A variable is anything that can be amended, added, removed or adapted within the deal. Price is just one such variable.

Both parties should work through how, by altering variables, the challenges can be overcome, and the success criteria achieved. Finding the best fit for both parties and their respective outcomes may require a degree of creativity, but the process is about working through these options together.

One element that could increasingly become incorporated into deals is **shared risk and reward**. The idea here is that suppliers will have 'skin in the game' with potentially lower up-front costs in return for bonuses paid out on the achievement of agreed customer goals.

Plan – Establish plan to gain approval to deal

Once the seller has reached an agreement, they need to plan what is required to make the deal happen. It is likely that contracts will need to be drawn up and approved by procurement or legal teams and any SLAs will need to be agreed and ratified. These should be clearly mapped out before the negotiation is complete and, where necessary, the seller should seek to understand and explore what potential objections there may be to the deal that they have forged and how such resistance can be overcome.

Execute – Agree specific actions and steps

The seller needs to ensure there is continued commitment to move forward. The key contact is on the fourth step of their buying journey (resolve concerns) and, despite agreement having been reached, there is still a hugely significant step that the customer needs to take before the deal is closed and the seller can work on implementation and achieving customer goals.

The basic premise is the same as it was following both the discovery and the pitch, the more *action* we can commit the customer to at this stage, and the more specific those actions are, the more certainty everyone has that the deal will move forward.

SELLING ON PRICE

In previous chapters, we highlighted the opposing strategies of gaining a competitive advantage based on price verses value and differentiation. Whilst there are organisations that are set up to primarily compete on price, this often proves problematic for the following reasons:

- There is a perception of commoditisation that makes differentiation more difficult.
- Price is reinforced as the main buying criteria, with customers expecting the same or a better deal next time.
- The seller is open to competitors leading with price to encourage their customers to switch.
- Continuing to compete on price, and the subsequent margin reduction, may lead to reduced service levels,

diminished value and a loss of focus on the customer's outcomes.

There can also be catastrophic consequences for customers who buy *solely based on price*. Cheaper components or lower levels of service can significantly increase long-term costs or lead to brand and reputational damage.

A common scenario in the construction sector, where margins are traditionally low, is the awarding of contracts to the lowest bidder, which could mean using cheaper materials and corners being cut. Worst case scenario, the contractor goes bust part way through a job, creating further delays, penalties and a whole re-tendering process resulting in projects going over budget. A case of short-term gain leading to long-term pain.

SELLING ON VALUE

Earlier, we defined **value** as the difference that the seller can offer and the size of the problem that this potentially solves.

Whilst there is increasing emphasis on cost control in the New World, the role of the Transformational Seller is to ensure that ROI (return on investment), 'lifetime value' and protection of the customer's business outweighs a 'lowest price wins' mentality.

'Value creation' takes place at every stage of the buying journey, whereas negotiation tends to occur at Stage 4, Resolve Concerns, which means that it is often mistakenly viewed in isolation. In reality, it is an integral part of the overall process. How well the earlier phases are conducted influences what happens at the latter stages.

However, just because the seller does a great job in building value, it doesn't mean negotiation won't occur. Buyers are often targeted to extract the maximum possible from suppliers and gain the best price for their business. Many have KPIs based solely on price reduction. Just as sellers can operate Transactionally or Transformationally, so we have seen the same divergence amongst the buying community.

Whilst there are those whose sole aim is to drive down supplier costs, others are focused on developing profitable partnerships with suppliers and fostering collaboration. Moving forward, Transformational Selling organisations will need to make tough decisions around the businesses they choose as partners.

Avoiding assumptions

Bryn: We once worked with a business which had grown organically from a value of £5m to over £100m in just three years. It sounds implausible, but this growth came about because they were awarded the worldwide rights to a now very well-established alcoholic drink which took off globally.

They were in the right place at the right time and were humble enough to understand this. They recognised that despite such great growth, their biggest challenge was to gain a better margin when dealing with large supermarket chains (not an easy task).

From our Discovery Phase, we identified that there was a lot of work to be done with their sales and leadership teams. Thus far, with a product that had exploded onto the market, their sales team had delivered incredible results, albeit through a transactional and quantitative approach – they had secured some huge deals but at a margin the client demanded.

Our first assumption was that despite their recent success, they were a down-to-earth business. Asking for a large investment might scare them off. Therefore, we proposed a contract that would at least start them on their journey without them baulking at the cost.

Their managing director came back to us shortly afterwards. He liked what we had proposed, with one exception. He didn't just want to start his sales team on the journey, he wanted to give them the full suite of skills they needed and asked us to re-cost the programme for double the amount of training.

In doing this, we had a dilemma as to whether we should include a price concession in the revised quote to recognise the increased order value. Our second assumption was that this was something that many customers expect.

We decided not to do this, if the customer did come back and request it, this was something we could work on. To our surprise they didn't request it, they signed and returned the contract for the full value.

The accompanying email explained why. Their managing director made reference to the fact that we hadn't offered a discount for greater volume stating that he saw that a positive. It meant that we would drive the importance of not capitulating to customers on price and that we ourselves would not be cutting any corners in our service.

TRADING IN A TRANSFORMATIONAL WAY

Traditionally, where money becomes tighter and budgets are harder to unlock, customers turn to negotiation to leverage more for less from their suppliers. The key response has been either to concede, or, for those suppliers in a stronger position or those with a more positive mindset, to start trading. In other words, if we alter this one aspect of the deal in the customer's favour, we will offset this by attempting to restore some form of balance the other way.

A typical trade may involve agreeing to a discount in return for the customer extending the contract period, or alternatively, waiving delivery charges in exchange for an increased order volume.

Whilst the concept of trading, as opposed to capitulation, has long been taught as part of the process, the emphasis to date has been on what we would describe as tit-for-tat negotiation. The customer wants something, so we ask for something in return.

Moving forward, the feel of this process needs to evolve, and the Transformational Seller must take control in managing this 'trading' as part of the **options** phase by:

- **Ascertaining what the customer really values** – questioning against the backdrop of the customer's stated outcomes. In other words, the seller focuses the discussion on how this concession supports the achievement of the outcomes.
- **Maintaining transparency** – ensuring that both parties in the relationship get what they need. The Transformational Seller will review how the customer concession impacts the achievement of the seller's own stated outcomes.
- **Getting creative** – making suggestions as to how best to achieve both outcomes either through mitigating the impacts of making the concession or identifying an alternative approach that enables both parties to achieve their objectives.

Trading the Transformational way

Imagine that the customer is pressing for a reduction in the monthly fee for a service contract. In this situation, the seller must first establish how gaining a cost reduction supports the required customer outcomes.

"You highlighted that your main cause for concern is ensuring that your network achieves a minimum of ninety-seven percent up-time over the next twelve months. If we were to offer a discount on the service contract, how would this better enable you to achieve your uptime targets?" – **ascertaining what the customer really values**

"I appreciate that a reduced fee would avoid you having to go back for further budget approval. The challenge with discounting the rate though is that it would eat into our ability to continue to invest in the upgrades to the service whilst still maintaining the required margin and profitability of the deal." – **maintaining transparency**

"To address the profitability issue, we could look at taking out some of the costs of providing such a service. There is a cost to us involved in setting you up which is reduced when spread over a two-year contract period rather than one... in addition another route would be for your technical team to conduct some of the up-front data gathering which will enable our team to conduct more of the initial analysis remotely." – **getting creative**

It's important that if organisations are to empower their sellers to have these conversations, that the 'commercials' are better understood. Part of the reason why sellers capitulate comes from a lack of understanding around the impact of their concessions.

For example, getting someone on site quickly and free of charge seems like it doesn't really cost much. However, it does if that individual's time is usually chargeable, or they have to come off another project with critical timeframes. Alternatively, offering ninety-day payment terms because your business is cash-rich can backfire if your customer goes bust on Day 89!

In more complex negotiations, you will need to recognise the 'rankings' of different variables and their impact on your business and profitability against the potential value each represents to the customer. This will involve collaborating and reviewing which of these provide the best way of achieving both parties' goals.

There are times where the customer values something that is especially costly for your organisation and therefore has a large impact on profitability. Highlighting this, and the cost impact, will do one of two things: it will cause the customer to re-evaluate whether it is vitally important or they will recognise the need to improve their offer as a result.

Collaboration works on the basis of trust and requires honesty with your customer. Just as you should be explicit around the additional costs that you could incur, you also need to be transparent with the variables which are easier for you to provide. Conventional wisdom has been to 'maximise' the perceived effort in providing the concession – customers place a greater value on something they believe you have had to work hard for.

In true collaboration, if something is easy to provide, then a large intake of breath whilst saying "that's going to be tricky, let me see what I can do" reverts back to the poker-playing negotiation paradigm. There is no place in the New World for such games.

Going forward, the stage is set for more 'shared risk and reward' ventures between customers and suppliers. If a customer needs a more favourable financial arrangement at the outset, it seems reasonable that the supplier should be able to negotiate a substantial bonus based on the success of the outcome be they increased sales, lower downtime, improved margins, long-term cost savings, improved manufacturing or logistics efficiency, savings on wastage etc. By focusing on outcomes, it is possible to negotiate supplier bonuses, whereas in the past emphasis has typically been solely focused on penalty clauses for failing to meet them.

ASSERTIVE DOES NOT MEAN AGGRESSIVE

The tone of a negotiation is vitally important. Once a negotiation becomes hostile and the gloves are off there is little chance of a settlement being reached.

'Glasnost', which means 'openness and transparency' enabled Mikhail Gorbachev and Western leaders to communicate in collaborative tones and feel comfortable doing business together, effectively ending the long Cold War.

The Good Friday Agreement in Northern Ireland was reached in the spirit of co-operation and culminated in a remarkable friendship between Martin McGuinness and Ian Paisley, despite them being from diametrically opposing sides of the political divide. No-one could have foreseen that happening during 'The Troubles', and this demonstrates what can happen when true collaboration and openness is offered by both sides.

Compromise is not a matter of 'giving something away': just as in any personal relationship, there is a need for both sides to be reasonable. If one party is doing all the compromising, it is likely to either lead to resentment, or a one-sided relationship, which creates the 'master-servant' dynamic. The spirit of collaboration the Transformational Seller fosters is critical in helping to reach a mutually agreeable and equitable solution. This means having honest conversations with customers focused on their desired outcomes.

By having a belief in what you sell, by discovering your customer's challenges, business goals and outcomes, demonstrating your expertise, and creating a solution which removes those obstacles to achieving success, the need to negotiate in the current traditional way will ultimately diminish, and when it does you should be well equipped with variables to trade other than price.

Exercise: Transformational Trading

Work on an existing prospect currently at the advanced stage, one which you are hoping to close.

Use the SCOPE Framework to understand what mutual success looks like (i.e., what the customer and the seller both require from the deal), what challenges both parties need to overcome, and the options available.

Next, plan your strategy and set up the next meeting to execute this. Dummy run this with a colleague.

CHAPTER SUMMARY

- The focus for many sales negotiations has thus far been built on a competitive rather than collaborative basis. In the New World, collaboration and partnership will be key and this will need to be reflected in the way that buyers and sellers negotiate deals.
- Capitulation is a common problem with sellers too eager to get the business often at a cost to their own organisation and themselves.
- The alternative to collaboration is the decision to walk away. Transformational Sellers recognise that if the customer isn't prepared to collaborate in the long term, then it's unlikely to become a profitable partnership.
- Collaborative negotiation can be structured using the same SCOPE Model that was previously utilised for effective discovery.
- The starting point for the negotiation process should be to review the **success outcomes** for both parties. Laying these out up front enables the rest of the negotiation to

focus on ensuring that it works towards a win-win for both parties.

- When reviewing the **challenges** each party may have, it's important that the seller questions (or explains) **why**. If the customer wants a discount, the seller needs to ask why a discount would better help them to achieve their stated outcomes.

- **Options** can be developed and discussed in relation to both the success outcomes and the challenges to develop ideas to ensure how best to achieve mutual outcomes.

- **Planning** how the proposed options will gain the necessary approval is important. If there is likely to be resistance from other parties who need to sign off the deal, then a plan needs to be developed as to how such resistance will be overcome.

- As with every aspect of the sales process, gaining active commitment to the **execution** of the plan is a vital, but frequently missed, component.

- Selling purely on price has many disadvantages and few advantages. If a seller wins a deal based on price, they will probably lose it on price further down the line. In addition, customers who simply want to cut costs can suffer irreparable reputational damage.

- Trading in a Transformational way is about working with the customer to ensure that both parties achieve their success criteria. It's not tit-for-tat horse trading, but about ascertaining what the customer really values, and then getting creative with the best ways of achieving the outcome.

- The Transformational Seller treats the customer as an equal and expects to be treated as an equal – a Transformational Seller is a true collaborator.

CHAPTER 14
GAINING ACTIVE COMMITMENT

You miss 100% of the shots you don't take.

Wayne Gretsky (Ice-Hockey's 'The Great One')

The film *Glengarry Glen Ross* embedded the ABC (Always Be Closing) mantra into the sales lexicon. Alec Baldwin's character, with his intimidating approach lectures a team of underperforming real estate sellers on the virtues of ABC. Despite his aggressive tone and the subsequent unethical approaches adopted by the team, this term has infiltrated its way into everyday parlance and conventional sales wisdom.

In our experience, **closing** has historically been the most sought-after skill by sales directors. We have all seen job advertisements stating 'closers wanted' although these tend to relate to sales operations at the Transactional end of the spectrum.

In the world of the Transformational Seller, closing is far more complex.

Firstly, we need to deal with the common misnomer that 'closing' simply means 'winning the deal'. In the multi-stage sales processes that the Transformational Seller follows, closing is about ensuring that, following each customer interaction, there is an agreed commitment and mutual next step firmly in place.

Secondly, in the world of B2B selling, it is increasingly rare (again outside the Transactional World) for a customer to commit to a purchasing decision in the presence of the seller. Decisions usually need to be ratified and approved with senior management or by procurement and legal teams. The idea that you can walk out of a customer's office with a signed contract is often folly.

Thirdly, although gaining commitment is part of the Transformational Seller's skill set, it's dependent upon the work that goes before. Whilst we have seen a myriad of approaches, closing is straightforward if the seller has done a thorough job up to that point. If they haven't, then irrespective of how good your closing technique is, it's unlikely to be successful.

In Chapter 11, we introduced our Belay Model, the importance of gaining customer agreement to 'mutual next steps' and the definition of **active** and **passive** commitment. For commitment to be 'active' the customer must agree to complete specific actions. So, the mantra is not so much 'Always Be Closing' as 'Always Be Gaining Active Commitment To Next Steps'. It's a shame that ABC is lot snappier than ABGACTNS!

Gaining active commitment

Bryn: In 2003, I launched a property business in Spain. In hindsight, this was my 'mid-life crisis venture' as when the market crashed, it cost me a a small fortune. It was very successful to start with though, and I learned some great lessons around gaining active commitment.

Active Commitment Lesson One

I had to establish whether people were genuinely interested in buying a property there. We created 'Inspection Trips' for people to view. We ran a lot of presentations at golf clubs (as this was a good demographic) and also exhibited at major overseas property shows which gave us increased footfall but also more competition.

If we couldn't convert at these events, they would be followed up by an appointment at the potential client's home – something I'd never experienced before. The aim was to qualify their needs and approximate budget and get a commitment to a trip. I was initially surprised at the high success rate, when compared with typical B2B conversion rates. It helped that they were committing to head off to the sun, but it was a good test of who was serious and who wasn't. Once out in Spain, the conversion rate to buying was around eighty-two percent!

As we became more established, there were an increasing number of potential clients I hadn't personally met before I greeted them at Malaga airport. Their first words after "hello" were often, "we want you to know that we aren't planning to buy on this trip."

This was when I learned the next lesson.

Active Commitment Lesson Two

Never try to coerce a customer at an early stage in the buying process (which many other agents did).

My reply would be: "It's ok, I'm not expecting you to buy on this trip, but can I just ask you one question: what's your main reason for coming out here to look?'

Gradually they would start to open up to me, even more so when I stated that we would visit just a handful of properties that day, after a drink at my golf club. As most people had a very early start to the day to catch their flight, it was important that they felt relaxed. We'd sit on the terrace enjoying the view in the sun long enough for their contented sighs to intimate, "we could get used to this". They were already making an active commitment to the lifestyle.

By the end of the second day of viewings and once again relaxed over a usually al fresco dinner, we would review their favourite properties and the conversation would invariably unfold thus: "you know that lovely development we saw today, well, we've been talking about it since you dropped us at the hotel. What would happen if we were interested in buying it?"

I'd remind them then that they said they weren't planning to buy on this trip, and they didn't need to feel under any pressure to do so. They would often become more insistent at that point and eventually, if they were 100% sure, we would make an appointment at the lawyer's office, take a small refundable deposit and take their chosen property off the market whilst the lawyers did all their checks.

We were never once asked to refund a deposit and we sold over 250 properties! I believe that this is because throughout the process the customer was the one making all the commitment, as opposed to me trying to apply pressure.

The rules around gaining commitment are universal: active commitment is far more effective when the client sees the importance and urgency of the situation, as opposed to having the sale foisted upon them. Aggressive sales tactics rarely work outside of the most Transactional settings, and when they do, they usually end with **buyer's remorse** in the form of returned deposits, cancelled orders or one-off sales.

GETTING COMMITMENT TO INVOLVE THE DMU

You've developed a good relationship with your key contact, but you need to get 'higher and wider' within the organisation. Whilst your contact will be pivotal to success, they will not be making this decision alone and may have limited influence over the rest of the DMU (i.e., the other stakeholders).

The first step is to gain their trust and acceptance to sponsor you into their colleagues. This can concern some sellers who believe, often erroneously, that attempting to do so could undermine your contact's authority and jeopardise the relationship. However, if they are genuinely interested, this step may well be essential in ensuring that you close the deal. Failure to gain access to the rest of the DMU relies on 'selling by proxy' without your input. Irrespective of what the 'reasons lost' might state in your CRM system, in our experience this is the number one reason for lost sales.

In order to gain access, whilst simultaneously remaining sensitive to the customer, you should look to follow the guiding Transformational principles of:

- **Focus on outcomes**
- **Leverage expertise**
- **Foster collaboration**

At this stage, you should have already identified the DMU and, through using the SCOPE Model for discovery, you should have also mapped out who and what needs to be involved in the next steps.

In this order the Transformational Seller:

Focuses on outcomes – summarises and agrees the outcomes that the customer wants to achieve as a result of moving forward with their offering. The use of questions and confirmation is key to re-affirming why this should be done.

Leverages expertise – reviews their understanding of the 'authority' within their BANT qualification, confirming the members of the DMU and the process required to gain approval. Then they need to leverage their expertise around:

- Previous experience of having to influence multiple stakeholders (e.g., "I know that getting everybody to buy into this can be a challenge").

- The challenges that are likely to come from these stakeholders (e.g., "I often find that CFOs tend to have most reservations when it comes to ... what do you think will be the main sticking points with your CFO?")

They will then suggest ways and ideas around how to strengthen the case with particular stakeholders: "I've found that these messages have been particularly useful in the past …".

Fosters collaboration – with their customer to come up with a plan: "How do we maximise our chances of getting the rest of the DMU on side, and what role do you need me to play?", "How do we ensure that we combine my expertise in the solution with your expertise of the business to get the result that we need?"

All of this provides a good litmus test for how interested your sponsor really is in recommending your solution, as well as helping you to understand who else is likely to be involved in making the decision. If the customer is reluctant to answer this key question, they are probably still unconvinced around the merits of your offering or their need for change.

DMUs generally involve decision makers, influencers and users, so even if your contact is the key person with the authority to make a decision, that should not prevent you from building wider sponsorship. Always remember that your contact may leave, retire, move to a different role, get fired or be made redundant. You can't rely on them indefinitely.

There will be other blockers to overcome, and these can occur at any stage.

HANDLING CUSTOMER RESERVATIONS – WORKING THROUGH THE FUD FACTORS

The problem with objection handling

At some point it's likely that you have been approached in the street by someone asking you for change for a cup of coffee, some food or perhaps their bus fare home. You may have told the individual, "I'm sorry I don't have any change", even though you do.

In effect, you lied. Why? Probably because it was the easiest way to kill the conversation. Most people don't want to get into a debate over whether they believe the person's story or why they might not feel comfortable giving a stranger their hard-earned cash. There are numerous reasons why we might choose not to give the money. It's often easier to lie.

This illustrates the problem with traditional objection handling. Sellers will often look for the perfect repost to a customer's objection; the statement that will instantly win the day and elicit the response: "You know what, I was wrong and you're right, let's do it!"

The reality is that customers don't always tell you the truth, particularly during the earlier stages of the process. Many objections are no more than white lies, fob-offs or deliberate conversation killers.

Even where there is a degree of truth within an objection, its root cause may not be clear. Take the objection: "that's too expensive!" What does that really mean?

It means one of the following:

- That's more than I have in my budget!
- That's more than I was expecting to pay!
- The benefit we get isn't worth that level of investment
- I've had a cheaper quotation.
- I like it but want to negotiate.

All of these answers mean something different and yet still get articulated as: 'too expensive'.

Therefore, the most important element of what is referred to as 'objection handing' is ensuring that you understand exactly what the customer's issue is and, perhaps more importantly, what steps you can take to prevent it from arising in the first place.

After all, just solving the problem for the customer at face value is the equivalent of the stranger overcoming the 'no change' objection by producing a card machine.

In the world of Transformational Selling, we prefer to use the term **reservations** rather than 'objections' or 'resistance'. The word 'objection' has negative connotations and reflects a more adversarial mindset when engaging with customers. The idea of 'objection handling' is combative terminology and less conducive to a collaborative approach.

Customer reservations can arise anywhere in the buying journey, and from a chronological perspective, don't fit specifically into any one section. So why incorporate them into a chapter entitled 'Gaining Commitment'? Isn't it a bit late? If the mantra is **Always Be Gaining Active Commitments To Next Steps**, then simultaneously we should also **Always Be Looking To Manage The Customer's Reservations**.

Removing the potential obstacles is a critical part of the sales process and understanding and dealing with them well are vital elements to successfully navigating your way through to the ultimate prize – a commercial relationship.

It is most unlikely that your client will have *no* reservations throughout the sales process and the most effective way of working through these is to encourage them to voice their reservations at *each stage of the journey*. For example, in the Discovery Phase it is important to understand where any potential blockers might sit so that you can construct a proposal or quotation that takes these into account rather than waiting until you have delivered your pitch. These should be explored during the plan phase of your SCOPE conversations (see Chapter 8).

During your pitch, you should look to establish the customer's agreement to your proposals, together with any areas they wish to challenge or are unsure about. Make it interactive and encourage questions throughout rather than at the very end (your competitor may already be waiting in Reception by that point).

Prevention is better than cure and pre-empting reservations before the customer raises them is invaluable if you want to take control of the situation and avoid reservations that lead to conflict. By asking whether the customer has some concerns over your ability to complete the project on time, the cost versus the stated budget or achieving the desired outcome might sound counter-intuitive, but there are sound reasons for asking these questions.

This method demonstrates a sense of empathy with the customer. It shows that you appreciate that the decision they are making is not always an easy one and that they – like other clients – are likely to experience FUD factors. You are also making it easier for the customer to raise nagging doubts by telling them that it's perfectly normal to have them.

Chris Voss' book *Never Split the Difference* talks about the use of an 'accusation audit'. He believes that highlighting the negative things that someone could say about you or your offering, bringing them to the fore, lessens their impact and enables issues to be resolved.

With this in mind, we have looked at the most common root causes for reservations and FUDs and identified how these can be managed throughout the buying journey. Notice how all of these approaches capitalise on the three fundamentals: **outcomes**, **expertise** and **collaboration**.

ROOT CAUSE OF CUSTOMER RESERVATION – THE FIVE MOST COMMON FUDS

FUD Number One – Poor Customer Experience

This doesn't necessarily mean that their experience with you, your company or product has been poor. It might be a wider issue of experience with other providers.

Whatever the 'experience' the customer is referring to, the seller needs to focus the customer on how they intend it to be different this time. The first question should be: "why do you think it didn't work last time?"

This naturally starts the focus of attention around what should be different this time. Typically, a poor experience will be down to: a product/service being sold which wasn't fit for purpose or was implemented poorly; or else there was a misalignment of customer expectations. We find that when a customer points to a poor previous experience, they often apportion some of the blame to themselves: "we didn't implement it well" or "we didn't get buy in ...".

Whatever the reasons, the seller has the opportunity to leverage their own expertise. They might be able to guide the customer with questions or observations that will help them to understand why it might not have worked last time, for example:

- "One thing that we stress is the importance of gaining buy-in from the users up front. How did you go about doing that last time? What support did your supplier provide?

- I know from speaking with other businesses that there can often be a lot of functionality that doesn't quite work for your company. What discussions did you have around adapting these to better fit your business?"

Both of these questions re-emphasise the importance of collaboration and the role of the supplier in working with their customer to ensure that they achieve their goals. (Remember the important shift in the seller's horizons in aligning them to the customer's horizons?)

The next step would be to focus the discussions around how this time it will be different:

- What has been different about the conversations that we've been having?
- How different is the emphasis on your outcomes this time as opposed to last time?

This naturally leads the seller into the conversations around the plan as to how the seller proposes to ensure success this time around.

The service break-down paradox

There's a common limiting belief we hear from sellers that customers won't deal with them due to previous service, product or communication issues. What they often fail to appreciate is that every supplier has problems from time to time and most clients recognise this. The issue is more about how the seller subsequently reacts to and resolves them which impacts the customer's perception.

Studies have shown that customer loyalty following a problem or disruption, when dealt with swiftly and effectively, can actually increase. In other words, you can have higher customer loyalty after it goes wrong compared to a situation where everything had worked perfectly.

FUD Number Two – Happy with Existing Supplier/Solution

As we have stated throughout this book, customers are naturally hesitant to change. Changing is associated with a perception of risk, hassle and 'the grass is not always greener' type thinking.

Sellers don't always ask why an incumbent was selected, what their customer's involvement was in the process, or even what they like about them (perhaps through fear of hearing something positive). Therefore, they are unable to build up an accurate picture of the customer's satisfaction level, or erosion thereof.

In these circumstances, the Transformational Seller focuses the conversation back to the customer's outcomes and challenges (as per the SCOPE Model). The typical mistake is focusing the conversation on the product or service and what the customer would change about the current arrangements. Whilst that can work, often the customer just asks for a 'slightly faster horse'.

The real driver for the customer is the 'gap' between the success they desire and the impact that the challenges will have on them being able to achieve it. If there are FUDs around making the change, then the Transformational Seller needs to elevate the FUDs of *not* making the change.

FUD Number Three – In No Rush To Do Anything

The 'stall' can be extremely frustrating and is likely to surface with greater frequency in the New World. Not just with customers who are consolidating or being cautious, but even as confidence improves, increased complexity of decision making and the DMU will impact the speed with which decisions are made.

The Transformational Seller creates a compelling reason to change, leveraging their expertise to illustrate how the customer will benefit and subsequently achieve their outcomes. There is often a cost to *not* making a decision, and many businesses fail or go backwards because of such indecision.

The key is to first establish whether this is a genuine issue of timing or to express that a solution doesn't need to be found immediately. The seller should establish whether it is genuinely a "yes, but not right now" scenario or a "we might want to do something in the future" one. They could ask the customer to run through the business case for adopting the seller's solution and then gauge the customer's appetite or desire to make it happen. The other way – and in the spirit of collaboration this may be more effective – is simply to ask directly: "is it a case of 'if' rather than 'when'?"

If the customer is uncertain, then the seller needs to follow similar steps to the 'happy with existing supplier' scenario and help them to build the business case. Reviewing their success criteria and the challenges in achieving them creates the gap and a compelling reason for change.

If it's a genuine case of 'when' rather than 'if', then the seller needs to go back to the plan stage of the SCOPE Model and investigate further. They will need work through the backward plan in terms of:

- When does the customer need to see the results from this change?
- How long will it take to implement and ramp up the impact of the solution?
- What are the typical lead times that everyone is working to?

- When does the contract need to be signed or the order need to be placed?

Then, and perhaps most importantly, the discussion needs to revolve around:

- What is the cost or impact for each month that this is delayed?

An interesting word that came out of the pandemic was **pivot** which led to the need for both businesses and individuals to adapt quickly. This term will continue to be the watchword moving forward, and companies who are consistently able to flex and adapt will be the ones that survive and thrive. In short, this is Darwin's Theory in action (see Introduction).

FUD Number Four – No Previous Experience of Working With The Seller

This adds another dimension, especially if you are new to the market, have an innovative product or service, or if the customer has never heard of you before.

In each case, you will create a perceived degree of risk to the client. However, on the flip side, you also present a new and unique opportunity to them. We have seen how well some 'disrupter' brands in various markets have changed the way we do business. Companies such as Airbnb, Uber, Deliveroo, and more recently Zoom have taken off as people discovered alternatives to more traditional offerings.

At this point, the obvious solution is to provide the customer with some reassurances. There is no doubt that the use of case studies, testimonials and specific customer references are all valuable as they give the customer confidence and help build your brand and reputation. Demonstrating through formal case studies and informal story-telling, particularly where these provide specifics around outcomes and how they were achieved, goes a long way. As we stated previously, getting your prospect to speak to one of your existing customer's is often very powerful in providing the comfort they need.

However, the Transformational Seller is acutely aware that, as with other reservations, this may only be part of the problem. Before calling in a favour from an existing customer you need to be sure that this isn't just the equivalent of "I haven't got any change".

You need to walk back through the discovery process and ensure that either the erosion of satisfaction or the compelling event are truly strong enough for the customer to commit to some form of action. You may even need to repeat your questioning and ensure that you have adequately reviewed the impact not making the change could have on the achievement of the customer's outcomes.

FUD Number Five – You're Too Expensive

It would be extremely remiss of us to leave out the one we hear many times over.

As we explored earlier, concerns over money can manifest themselves in many ways, but as with all approaches to overcoming reservations, we refer back to a combination of focus on outcomes, leverage expertise and foster collaboration.

With this in mind, the typical steps that you will need to take will include:

Understand the root cause – in the spirit of collaboration, encourage your customer to elaborate on their financial reservations. Are they driven by an expectation of what the cost should be for your offering? Ask where they got that idea from. Is it based on their budget, or the potential financial benefits that they anticipate will result from the purchase?

Creating or reviewing the business case – review the customer's potential outcomes, the level of investment and the return they might expect. Whilst we can't usually predict exact results, we can work with the customer to establish what a realistic set of outcomes could be and the assumptions made when arriving at them. You may need to monetise some of the intangibles: what does an increase in speed or response time mean financially to the customer? In technology terms what would *not* having the very best security or most reliable network mean in terms of reputational damage?

Assess the risk – products or services are rarely extremely cheap *and* simultaneously highly effective. Clients usually need to compromise either on price or quality and compromising on quality can prove to be risky and costly, so their perception of risk may need to be redefined or brought to the fore by the seller.

Change the currency – this fundamentally comes down to the great value versus price debate. However, the main factor that most customers and sellers miss is that the price or cost is an investment which is necessary to achieve an outcome. Often the conversation take place in absolute terms of a monthly cost or a one-off capital investment based on an input provided rather than linking it the outcomes. Instead of X dollars per month, it could be represented as Y dollars per one percent performance improvement.

Increasingly in the New World, changing the currency will be the approach that the Transformational Seller takes. The **shared risk and reward concept** is the ultimate example of this.

THE PROCESS FOR GAINING ACTIVE COMMITMENT

In a Transactional sale, the **close** includes some form of technique, designed to get the customer to say yes. There's the **assumptive close** ("shall we complete the paperwork now?"), the **alternative close** ("would you prefer to pay up front or spread the cost on a monthly basis?") and the **caution close** ("we only have a couple left in stock, can I go ahead and place the order now?"). There are also several other variations.

The Transformational Seller is not so concerned about these approaches as the process for them is not about getting the customer to say 'yes', it's about getting the customer to say what they are going to do next.

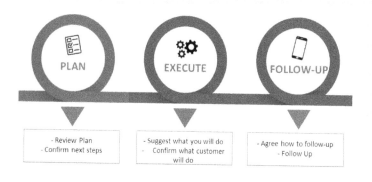

Figure 14.1: Process for Gaining Active Commitment © Sarah Morris

Process for gaining active commitment: an example

Plan

"According to the timeline, the next step will be to present our proposal at the committee meeting next month." **Confirming the Next Steps**

"We need to make sure that the proposal is as good as it can be and reflects the different needs and perspectives of the various committee members."

Execute

"To make our proposal compelling, it would be beneficial for us to speak with the different committee members so we can better understand what their perspectives are likely to be and we can then reflect this in the proposal" **Stating what we will do.**

"Can you set up calls with the committee and the make the necessary introductions" **Confirming what we need our customer to do.**

Follow-up

"When do you think you will be able to get those set up?"

"In that case, can we speak at the end of the week, and you can provide a little more background on each individual to help us prepare for those conversations"

Note how this final stage also doubles up as a deadline / follow up to ensure that our customer has completed the task that we asked of them?

FOLLOW-UP PROCESS

The key to gaining active commitment throughout the sales process is, wherever possible, to agree mutual actions either in the meeting or on the call. We are all familiar with those meetings where the minutes are distributed a week later and someone says: "that's not my understanding of what we agreed!"

Therefore, the 'verbal handshake' is extremely important as most people hate going back on their word. Anthony Robbins, the US business guru, tells a story about how a lawyer was trying to subpoena him for a court case he wanted to avoid attending, and when he eventually agreed on a date the lawyer asked him whether he had 'his word on this'. Robbins knew that once said that he did, there was no getting out of it. For the vast majority of people their word is their bond. It is a measure of trust and integrity.

Whilst asking the question, "do I have you word on that?" is perhaps too direct, you can nevertheless use alternative language to ensure they fulfil their part of the active commitment process. A 'summary close' is a good technique to ensure both parties are aware of their commitment obligations.

Summary close: an example

"So, to summarise what we've agreed: I will prepare a proposal in line with the parameters discussed.

(Re-state the parameters.)

You will set up a meeting a week on Tuesday at 10am with your boss and the head of operations, and I'll bring along our project manager.

If for any reason your colleagues can't make that date, we will re-schedule this to a week on Friday at 2.00pm when you know they will all be there for the monthly senior management meeting.

Are we agreed on that?"

Once this is confirmed you need to send an invitation to all parties, with an agenda attached in the body of the invitation, asking if there is anything else the customer wants to discuss, thus ensuring all parties' interests are covered.

The speed in which that invitation is accepted by the client is often a key indicator as to their level of interest: i.e., if this is done straightaway and by all parties you know they are keen to meet again and your chances of success are probably high.

Exercise: Gaining Active Commitment

Consider a sales opportunity you are currently engaged with and where you are about to engage on a next step (that may be a discovery call, a pitch, meeting with additional stakeholder etc).

Consider the following:

- What are the potential next steps following your interaction?
- What Active Commitment does this involve for the customer?
- What additional examples of Active Commitment could you gain from your customer that would increase their investment and equity in the process?
- What are you minimum and maximum objectives for this next interaction?

Incorporate these questions into your planning and preparation for all of your customer engagements.

CHAPTER SUMMARY

- **Closing** and **gaining commitment** is more than just 'clinching the deal'. In the Transformational world with multi-stage sales processes, it's the act of ensuring that after each intervention with the customer a clear and actionable next step is agreed.
- **Active commitment** requires **action**, and therefore effort on the customer's part. If the customer is unwilling to make any effort or go to any inconvenience, then you would have to question their level of commitment to the process.

- Gaining access to other members of the DMU is a prime example of the active commitment the Transformational Seller may be looking for. Using the principles of **focusing on outcomes, leveraging your expertise** and **fostering collaboration** the seller should look to develop a plan and strategy with their key contact for engaging with and gaining buy-in from the rest of the DMU.
- 'Objections' and 'resistance' are outdated terms in the Transformational World and reflect a more confrontational mindset towards sales. We refer to customer reservations and the need to help the customer work through their (FUDs) **fears, uncertainties** and **doubts**.
- The Transformational Seller draws out potential reservations throughout the sales process so that they can explore and deal with them once brought out into the open.
- Prevention is better than cure and the Transformational Seller works to ensure that the **compelling event** or **erosion of satisfaction** is strong enough to ensure the customer commits to seeing the process through to completion.
- There is no quick-fire technique or gimmick to helping the customer through their FUDs. We examined five typical examples and the importance of understanding the nature of the customer's reservations and showed how focusing on outcomes, leveraging expertise and fostering collaboration were key to working through each of these.
- The process of securing active commitment involves reviewing the plan, agreeing the seller's and the customer's role in the execution of next steps and agreeing how these will be followed up.

SUMMARY

During the writing of this book, one thought has been nagging away: are we being too harsh on those fellow sales professionals who are likely to make up the bulk of our potential readers? Are we biting the hand that could feed us?

Thinking back to our early sales careers, we were also afflicted by so many of the bad habits we have written about, and although we mention a few anecdotes of where we have achieved some notable successes, we would need a whole new book to write about the numerous failures we've also experienced along the way!

For the past fifteen years we have trained thousands of sellers across every continent: many of whom had been in sales for years and yet for a large proportion this was their first experience of sales training: how crazy is that?

Despite all the criticism, our affection for the people we've had the privilege of training is exceptionally strong. Most are decent hard-working people who throw themselves enthusiastically into each learning exercise, are prepared to hold their hands up and laugh at themselves when they make mistakes, and genuinely appreciate not just the steep learning curve that they go through on each course, but also the openness to change their approach.

One delegate really sticks out. He was quiet and reserved throughout the program, and despite his excellent product knowledge, we had reservations over whether he would develop as a result of the training.

As part of the follow up, we contacted him three months later, concerned to see how things were progressing:

"Un-be-lieve-ably" came the loud and highly animated reply. For a moment we thought we'd called the wrong person, this wasn't the shrinking violet we recalled from the classroom.

He continued: "My biggest takeaway from the program was that I needed to be much bolder. So, I went into the next meeting with a large rail company and opened with: 'I appreciate that there is a lot of testing and compliance required to win this contract, but if I can understand exactly what you are looking to achieve and can put together a solution that delivers your required results, will you work with me?."

He said the client was a little taken aback at this approach but admitted that if this was the case, he would indeed stand a very good chance. He told us that nine weeks and several meetings later, he walked away with a E350,000 contract.

We've won many deals and led some exceptional sales teams over the years but this remains one of the most significant highlights.

It proves that sellers aren't simply born, they need to develop. Of course, it helps if you have a personality that is suited to such a profession: highly driven; a natural confidence; good communication and rapport building skills; coupled with great resilience; tenacity; and a positive mindset.

However, sales is so much more than that: the structure and discipline you need to plan, set objectives, question, listen and qualify effectively, understand customer outcomes and focus your approach on how to achieve these. And having captured all this, be able to construct a backward plan, collaborate with your client and engage with multiple stakeholders to understand their diverse range of desires and motivations (including emotional drivers), leverage your expertise through your previous experiences of what has worked well and what hasn't, construct a relevant solution, overcome reservations, build value and constantly gain active commitment throughout the customer buying journey.

It's a long list, but these are skills that most people can learn and ultimately master. You don't need to be an extrovert, have 'the gift of the gab', or simply be 'a good closer' to be effective in sales, you need to follow a process thoroughly and methodically, be prepared to play the long-game and have an unshakeable belief in the value you can bring to help the customer to achieve their desired outcomes.

Sales is a tough profession, and it's never been tougher than right now in the New World and with the economic outlook for the foreseeable future. It is going to take a new approach, one that really benefits customers and suppliers alike, to succeed. We are already seeing customers looking to reduce fees, negotiate much harder and drive prices down from suppliers, but is that really the approach that is going to help them to achieve their outcomes? And are they really the customers you want to collaborate with?

The more that products and services move from ownership to subscription the greater the need for sellers to stick around and support the implementation. Whilst organisations may have delivery teams, customer experience managers and client account managers for implementation, the seller's absence following the initial signing of the order creates a disconnect for both the customer and the seller alike.

If the revenue and profitability of a deal for a selling organisation is dependent upon successful implementation, adoption and ultimately the customer's achievement of outcomes, then the seller's remuneration and personal outcomes will need to be aligned to this. Successful and proactive sellers will not want to see months of work fail to deliver outcomes for their customers and, by extension, themselves and so will drive the whole process through to completion, rather than sitting patiently on the side lines.

This creates a virtuous cycle for sellers, businesses and customers alike. The more that sellers are involved with the implementation and adoption phases the greater their insight and knowledge becomes. This expertise can then help grow and develop the relationship moving forward and realise the commercial opportunities that can result. Simultaneously, it also can be leveraged with other customers to better support them at all stages within their buying journey.

This drives further collaboration between the two parties. When both sides are focused on the same end result, it automatically changes the whole nature of the conversation and interactions between them.

We have pioneered working with customers on a 'Shared Reward Model' whereby we flexed our fees in return for an outcome focused bonus. In almost all cases we achieved the outcomes the client wanted and received some substantial bonuses in return. Both parties had 'skin in the game' which is usually the basis for true collaboration, and we see such arrangements becoming more prevalent in the future.

Genuine collaboration over the next few years is going to be vital to business performance and will prevent many sellers from going the way of the dinosaur. It will also ensure a lot of companies don't go to the wall either, so it really is in **both parties' interests** to focus on outcomes, leverage each other's expertise, and foster long lasting and collaborative partnerships.

In short, practising Transformational Selling transforms your sales results and, in turn, your customer's business.

Enjoy the journey.

APPENDIX A: TIER 1 QUALIFICATION: BANT

BUDGET

- How are budgets typically allocated?
- What flexibility is there in the budget?
- Has the budget been ring-fenced for this project or is it from a central post?
- If a budget has been put forward, how did they arrive at the figure, what assumptions have they made and what research went into identifying the budget?
- Who owns the budget, who is the budget holder?
- What does the budget approval process look like within the organisation?
- What are the limits of authority across different decision makers?

AUTHORITY

- Who are the different individuals and groups likely to be involved within the decision?
- What is the relative influence that each of these will have over the decision making process?
- What are the different 'interests' that each is likely to have in the purchase decision?
- What is the format and process by which the decision will be made?

Budget   **Authority**   **Need**   **Time**

NEED

- What are the outcomes that the customer is looking to achieve?
- What is the strategic importance of delivering these outcomes?
- What is the **compelling event** or **erosion of satisfaction**?
- What are the potential consequences if the need is not addressed?
- How well does the customer recognise the need (and how does this differ across the DMU)?
- How well does the specification requested deliver the customer's overall outcomes?

TIME

- When does the customer need to achieve their outcome?
- How flexible is the customer's deadline?
- What's driving this timescale and how flexible is it?
- What are the key milestones and timeframes regarding implementation?
- What is the lag between implementation and achievement of results/outcomes?
- What are the key milestones and timeframes regarding the decision-making process?

WHAT IS THE OPPORTUNITY?

APPENDIX B: TIER 2 QUALIFICATION: CASE

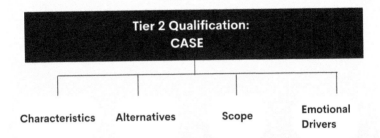

CHARACTERISTICS

- What are the different characteristics on their wish list?
- Why are these different characteristics important to them?
- What assumptions have they made in defining their wish list?
- How does the wish list and the priority order vary between different stakeholders within the DMU?

ALTERNATIVES

- What alternatives are the customer looking at?
- What other suppliers are they speaking to?
- What's their experience been like with other suppliers?
- How do they feel that your proposition stacks up in comparison (both in terms of what they like and what concerns they have)?
- What do they particularly like about what they have seen from the competition?
- What concerns or issues do they have with what they have seen from the competition?
- What's worked well and not so well with their incumbent supplier?

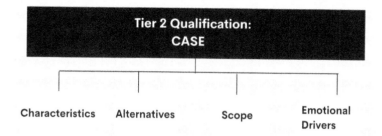

Tier 2 Qualification:
CASE

Characteristics   Alternatives   Scope   Emotional Drivers

SCOPE

- What scope is there for creating a stronger and more strategic business relationship?
- What are the opportunities both up and downstream from this one?
- What broader opportunities could this open the door to?
- To what extent can we differentiate by demonstrating a broader approach to enabling the customer to achieve their outcomes?
- What strategic significance does this opportunity represent for us?

EMOTIONAL DRIVERS

- How important is the achievement of their outcomes to them personally (i.e., sense of achievement, rewards, security, career etc.)?
- What is frustrating or concerning them most?
- How do these emotional drivers differ for each of these stakeholders within the DMU?
- What risks are associates within making this change?
- What are the potential FUD factors that are likely to be impacting their decision making?

HOW DO WE WIN IT?

AFTERWORD

Peter Ueberroth was *Time Magazine*'s Man of the Year in 1984. Despite being familiar with the result of his work and legacy most people have never heard of him.

What's so special about his achievements? He revolutionised the Olympic Games when, as Chairman of the Los Angeles Olympic Committee, he created the first privately financed Games, making an incredible $250m surplus and changing the face of modern-day sports sponsorship forever.

The previous three Olympics had all been blighted by huge controversies, financial disasters and human tragedies. The 1972 Munich Olympics will be remembered forever for the tragic murder of 11 Israeli athletes, coaches and judges by the Black September Terrorist Group.

The Montreal Olympics in 1976 was a fiscal nightmare: the Olympic Stadium was originally budgeted at $250m and ended up costing $1.4 billion! 'The Big O' as it was termed, soon became known as 'The Big Owe': it took 30 years of public money to pay off the debt, almost bankrupting the City. Today it's a skateboard park. To make matters even worse, 22 African

Nations boycotted the games that year due to the New Zealand rugby tour of apartheid South Africa.

Boycotting continued to dominate the games, with 66 countries refusing to participate at the 1980 Moscow Olympics, led by the USA objecting to the Soviet invasion of Afghanistan. The official IOC report on those games indicates an expenditure of $1.35 billion against revenues of $231million. An Oxford Olympics Study calculated the estimated cost in today's terms as $6.3billion.

So, given that the previous two Olympics made net losses of well over $1billion, how did Ueberroth magically transform the LA games into a quarter of a billion surplus? He did three things exceptionally well.

1. **Focused on Outcomes** – he knew that the first US based Summer Olympics for over 50 years would be a golden opportunity for sponsors to reach out to a global market and created exclusive brand categories for a select number of companies. Only one company per category could win, and in the first one he pitted Coca Cola against Pepsi on a 'sealed bid' basis, winner takes all. When he opened the Coca Cola envelope he said "I just loved all those zeros".

In film sponsorship he knew that Fuji, the Japanese giant and then number two in the world, were desperate to break into the US market to compete with Kodak. When Fuji made a winning bid of $5m, Kodak panicked and offered to substantially increase their previous offer, but it was too late: their one chance was gone, along with several senior Kodak employees!

Ueberroth had been given a highly demanding target of $116m in sponsorship revenue: he achieved $123m.

2. **Leveraged Expertise** – he understood both sport and business. In high school he excelled at baseball, football and swim-

ming, and received an athletics scholarship to San Jose State University, graduating with a degree in Business. He became VP of Trans International Airlines aged just 22, then founded his own travel company, First Travel Corporation, and grew it to become the second largest in North America.

He moved the goalposts with regard to funding the Olympics, turning a taxpayers' nightmare into a sponsor's dream: 156 countries filmed the 1984 Olympics, and 4.8 billion viewers tuned in.

3. **Fostered Collaboration** – Ueberroth was an extremely smart guy with a great eye for innovative thinking, but he recognised that he couldn't do it alone. He created a committee of 150 members (mostly business people and entrepreneurs) to generate ideas and opportunities, and to solve problems.

He also noticed on frequent visits to 7-Eleven stores that there were always lots of bicycles parked outside, so he contacted the company and persuaded them to sponsor the building of the LA Velodrome. This ultimately led to 7-Eleven starting its own cycling team, turning professional and competing successfully for many years in the Tour de France and Giro Italia.

Peter Ueberroth may well have been the first ever Transformational Seller.

GLOSSARY OF TERMS

Active Commitment: where the client commits to a specific action such as agreeing to send information, attending the next meeting, getting other stakeholders involved, etc.

Action Zone: where a seller is adopting a proactive approach (see **Comfort Zone** for opposite approach).

AI: Artificial Intelligence. For example, chatbots which are starting to replace humans in Transactional Sales.

Backward Plan: part of the SCOPE Framework for conducting an end-to-end sales process, the Backward Plan involves working backwards from where the customer achieves their desired outcomes, to all the steps that need to happen before then to ensure success. The key is in mutually agreed next steps (see **Active Commitment**).

Balance of Change: the aim of the Transformational Seller is to 'tip the scales' so that the balance moves from the customer from 'Fear of Changing' to 'Fear of Not Changing' (see **Catalyst for Change**).

BANT: Budget, Authority, Need, Timeframe – stage one qualification to determine the value (or otherwise) of spending time on the opportunity.

Belays: effectively anchors at each stage of the sales process (like those a climber installs to prevent themselves from falling) to ensure they continue to progress a sale (involves Active Client Commitment).

B2B Sales: Business-to-business sales as opposed to business-to-consumer (B2C) sales.

CASE: Characteristics, Alternatives, Scope, Emotional Drivers. The second stage qualification process after BANT (Stage 1 Qualification) which defines the Win Strategy.

Catalyst for Change: a Transformational Seller's goal is to change a prospect's mind, either by getting them to switch from their existing supplier or through purchasing a new product or service from them.

C-Suite/CEO/CRO/CTO/COO: Chief Executive Officer, Chief Revenue Officer, Chief Technical Officer, Chief Operating Officer. Generally, decision-makers operating at board level or just below.

Coach/Coachee: In a very similar way to a manager coaching a seller, through an 'asking not telling' process the seller (or coach) gets the customer (or coachee) to open up and self-reflect, with the ultimate aim of getting them to make a change.

Comfort Zone: a common trait found in sellers who wait for their customer to act as opposed to pro-actively engaging with them (see **Action Zone**). Very common in account management.

Commoditisation: when a product or service has little or no perceived differentiation from a competitor and the only real differentiators are price and availability.

Compelling Event: an event which mandates a client to act such as a change in legislation, a political event (e.g., Brexit) or a technological reason e.g., Y2K (see **Erosion of Satisfaction**).

Control Paradox: the sometimes mistaken belief that a seller is more in control when talking, pitching or demonstrating their product, as opposed to questioning and listening where they have far more control.

CRM: Customer Relationship Management (generic term for an IT system to track sales progress).

Customer Buying Journey: the process a customer goes through when making a purchase: Initial Interest; Establish Needs; Assess Options; Resolve Concerns; Commit to Action; Achieve Outcomes.

Differentiation: the unique or different aspects of the seller's solution that help them to create value (as opposed to price differentiation), sometimes referred to as USPs (see **USP**).

Discovery: the information a seller needs to extract from a client to understand their situation, the issues that got them on their buying journey, and the pain points that you ultimately aim to solve.

DMU: the decision making unit, i.e., a collection of decision makers, influencers and users who make up the stakeholder group commonly known as the DMU. 'Unit' may be a misnomer as they are not always fully aligned in what they desire from a purchase.

Enterprise Sale: a larger sale (sometimes described as 'big ticket') which generally takes longer to win and often involves multiple stakeholders and more complex processes.

Emotional Drivers: research suggests that up to 84% of decisions made are emotional, and the more emotion a client or prospect can feel the more they are likely to act and make a decision.

Erosion of Satisfaction: the most common reason why a client looks to buy or change (as opposed to a Compelling Event). This usually takes longer to realise, hence the seller's job is to create more urgency.

Event Horizon: the way different sellers view the end point of a sale. Traditionally this has been when the order is placed (Transactional), or where the problems are solved (Consulta-tive). For the Transformational Seller, it is when the client achieves their desired outcomes.

Focus on Outcomes: a Transformational Seller is concerned with the desired outcomes their customer is looking to achieve, and in doing so moves the conversation away from price and towards value.

Foster Collaboration: another of the three pillars of Transfor-mational Selling, the aim being to treat the customer as an equal, involving them throughout the process and agreeing mutual commitments at each stage (see **Active Commitment**).

Four Level Differentiation: the four ways a business can differ-entiate itself from their competitors: Core Product; Service Wrapper; Organisational Capability; Sales Approach.

FUDs: Fears, Uncertainties and Doubts. In traditional sales thinking they would be referred to as objections, however a Trans-actional Seller sees FUDs as perfectly natural and welcomes them before allaying the customer's fears, uncertainties and doubts.

Future Pacing: the point where the client has gone beyond a point where they are likely to turn back on their buying journey and the order is within sight.

Happy Ears: a slang term for over-optimistic sellers who forecast deals that often have little chance of landing as they have usually not created enough Active Commitment. Sometimes done in desperation.

HR: Human Resources. Over the years they have become increasingly influential and may well hold budgets for training, hence could form an integral part of the DMU (see also **Learning and Development**).

ICP: Ideal Customer Profile. The prospects sellers should be aiming to target based on the market they are in and their likely propensity to be interested in and in a position to be able to make a purchase.

Insights: ways in which the seller can leverage their expertise to help them prospect solve issues or challenges based on their past experience or similar situations.,

KPI: Key Performance Indicators. The measures by which most roles are targeted to ensure the business achieves its overall goals and business objectives

Labrador Effect: a metaphorical phrase for the seller who does everything to please their client whilst asking for nothing in return, akin to the Labrador dog who always bringing back the slipper with or without necessarily getting any reward for their labour.

L&D: Learning and Development. In larger businesses these could be stand-alone functions, in smaller ones they may form part of an HR department or fit within another division.

Leverage Expertise: another of the three pillars of Transformational Selling, which involves utilising the seller's industry experience based on what has worked well with other customers and highlighting some of the pitfalls the customer needs to be aware of before making their decision.

Limiting Beliefs: the often-fixed beliefs that sellers can have around prospecting, cross-selling, getting higher and wider in organisations that hold them back from being more successful.

Monetisation: the way a problem or issue could be monetised to see exactly what it is costing a client, or alternatively.

New World: the business world post-pandemic as viewed by the authors, and how this will affect the way we engage with clients and prospects in future.

PESTLE: Political, Economic, Social, Technical, Legal, Environmental. All issues that could be affecting businesses at any given time, and by raising relevant ones the seller has a better chance of engaging.

Present/Past/Future/Change Questioning: a pre-selected order of questioning to ascertain where the client is at now (in terms of desired outcomes versus actual), where they have been previously, where they would like to be in the future, and what needs to change as a result. Designed to create urgency once the customer realises they are not where they need to be and therefore require changes to be made.

Qualification Process: the process a seller should go through to question and understand whether or not the opportunity is realistic (Tier 1 BANT) and worth investing time in (if so, progress to Tier 2 Qualification focused on 'how do we win it?' – see **CASE**).

Questioning from Outside to In: by first examining the facts this technique then moves to understanding the issues and ultimately the impact of these issues if they remain unresolved. Helps to create a call to action.

SAAS: Software as a Service. Usually, a monthly type of contract many software businesses now apply to build up monthly and annual recurring revenue (MRR and ARR). Other derivations include IAAS (Infrastructure as a Service) and PAAS (Platform as a Service).

SCOPE: a new sales process. Success Outcomes, Challenges, Options, Plan, Execute. The aim is to initially widen the gap between the S and C to create urgency, then close it with the right options.

SDE: Set the scene, deliver (the insight), explore. A way of engaging a client through story-telling, ensuring that the case study or story is relevant and contextual the client's own situation.

SDR: a sales development representative, usually tasked with converting leads generated to meetings or demonstrations booked for more senior sellers, although some SDRs also sell directly.

Seven Conditions for Selling: the level or degree of need, complexity, risk, effort, commoditisation, decision-making and standardisation or otherwise in any sales situation.

SLA: Service Level Agreement. Often written into contracts so that both sides can measure how well the levels are being adhered to.

Stakeholders: the people in a company involved in the decision-making process (see **DMU**). They may comprise a mix of decision-makers, influencers, sponsors, detractors and end-users.

Story-telling: the art of using relevant stories or case studies to increase credibility and build trust, using the Quest – Conflict – Action – Result method.

TCT Spectrum: Transactional, Consultative and Transformational Selling defined. Indicates how to move from the left (Transactional) to the right (Transformational) to avoid extinction in the New World.

Transformational Expertise: the combination of product/service knowledge; industry experience and customer understanding used collectively to enable the seller to act as a Transformational Seller.

Transformational Mindset: the three key assets: expertise, skills and mindset, which need to be harnessed collectively to become a Transformational Seller.

Transformational Selling: based on the three core pillars: Focus on Outcomes, Leverage Expertise, Foster Collaboration. This is effectively a 'Super-Consultative' form of selling.

USP: Unique Selling Point, otherwise known as key differentiators.

Urgency to Act: accelerating the erosion of satisfaction; in the prospect's mind so that they make faster decisions in favour of the seller.

Value: defined as the Perceived Difference x Problem Solved.

Value Added Supplier: the ability of a seller to demonstrate value as opposed to selling purely on price.

Win Themes: used when pitching or presenting, starting with differentiators, identifying customer challenges and demonstrating successful outcomes.

20-40-40: the approximate percentages sellers should be working towards when delivering pitches, presentations and demonstrations. 20% summarising the situation and key challenges, 40% pitching or demonstrating, and the final 40% to gain client feedback, discuss further and agree next steps.